W9-CXN-990

THE UNITED NATIONS AND THE MAINTENANCE OF INTERNATIONAL SECURITY

A Challenge to Be Met

Second Edition

JAMES S. SUTTERLIN

Foreword by Bruce Russett

Westport, Connecticut
London

Library of Congress Cataloging-in-Publication Data

Sutterlin, James S.
  The United Nations and the maintenance of international security : a challenge to be
met / James S. Sutterlin ; foreword by Bruce Russett—2nd ed.
      p. cm.
  Includes bibliographical references and index.
  ISBN 0–275–97297–6 (alk. paper)—ISBN 0–275–97304–2 (pbk. : alk. paper)
      1. Security, International.   2. United Nations.   3. United Nations—Armed Forces.
  I. Title.
  JZ5588.S88   2003
  341.5′8—dc 21   2002193037

British Library Cataloguing in Publication Data is available.

Copyright © 2003 by James S. Sutterlin

All rights reserved. No portion of this book may be
reproduced, by any process or technique, without the
express written consent of the publisher.

Library of Congress Catalog Card Number: 2002193037
ISBN: 0–275–97297–6
       0–275–97304–2 (pbk.)

First published in 2003

Praeger Publishers, 88 Post Road West, Westport, CT 06881
An imprint of Greenwood Publishing Group, Inc.
www.praeger.com

Printed in the United States of America

The paper used in this book complies with the
Permanent Paper Standard issued by the National
Information Standards Organization (Z39.48–1984).

10   9   8   7   6   5   4   3   2   1

CONTENTS

FOREWORD

Jim Sutterlin introduced himself to me in 1985. At that time he was executive director of the Executive Office of the Secretary-General of the United Nations—effectively the right-hand person to Javier Pérez de Cuéllar. Earlier he had served for eight years as director of the Political Affairs Division of the United Nations under Pérez de Cuéllar and the previous secretary-general, Kurt Waldheim. In those capacities he had witnessed both successes and failures in UN efforts to keep or restore the peace and had developed many ideas about how the office of the secretary-general, along with various other parts of the UN system, might be strengthened. He had the experience and the political sense to know it would not be easy. But he also—as few others of that time—had the intellectual vision to see some possibilities and to reach out to the academic community for advice in shaping that vision.

This was, however, at the height of the cold war—a time when the UN was even less highly valued than now by many policymakers, and when most academic scholarship had turned away from global institutions. I myself had not done serious scholarship on the United Nations for almost two decades. In coming to academics in general, and to us at Yale in particular, Jim therefore had to prime a pump that was pretty dry. He did so by graciously seeking our advice even though he may not have expected much of immediate value in return, pulling several of us at Yale into his international network, and kindling or rekindling our interest in the possibilities of a stronger United Nations. In doing so he and some young colleagues from the Secretariat organized a series of international conferences in Multilateral Means of Reducing the Risk of War. Those conferences brought together scholars and policymakers who, perhaps to their surprise, found they had much to share, in terms of experience, ideas, and a growing sense that some enhancement of the UN's role in international peace and security might indeed be feasible.

Shortly thereafter Sutterlin retired from UN service and was free, as a private citizen, to pursue his ideas and convictions. In 1988 he became a fellow of the program in International Security Studies at Yale and began to pursue one of the most vigorous and productive "retirements" I have ever seen. Yale was extremely lucky to have this energetic policy intellectual in its midst. Yale and Sutterlin were both lucky, too, in timing. By then the cold war was breaking down. The Soviet Union and the United States began to cooperate more and started to see ways in which the United Nations might help to stabilize some of the political transformations that were beginning to occur. Use of the veto in the Security Council became rare, as the Permanent Members endorsed a wide range of new peacekeeping activities. "New thinkers" under Mikhail Gorbachev were especially open to ideas for enhancing the United Nations. Our international conferences became more wide-ranging, more innovative, and more productive. Many of us were drawn in by the new sense of intellectual excitement and the opportunity for strengthening international institutions.

The focus of our earliest discussions, on the possible role of the United Nations in crisis management, was appropriate to the mid-1980s, when so much attention was devoted to the risks of a Soviet-U.S. nuclear confrontation. Sutterlin's special contributions, however, were to explore ways in which the secretary-general's office might be strengthened both in its capacities for timely information gathering and in its ability to communicate rapidly in possible mediation with crisis participants. Distinctive also was his concern about multilateral crises, not just because confrontations between small powers might bring the two nuclear superpowers into conflict, but because such confrontations might also bring in other nuclear powers, in a much more complex and dangerous interplay than a straight bipolar conflict would imply.

As these fears eased somewhat with the end of the cold war, he was quick to see that the possible—and necessary—role of the United Nations was much broader. The UN in its most visible manifestations had been focused on collective security enforcement (uniquely, before 1990, in the Korean War) and on traditional peacekeeping; that is, as an impartial force operating with the permission of warring parties who were ready to cease fighting, most often in international conflicts. Sutterlin recognized that future conflicts were likely very often to be located within existing states rather than between them and to require a much wider range of international capabilities. The focus of a post–cold war United Nations, he realized, should be on *human security*—not just the security of the states that are members of the United Nations, but the security of populations within states. Transitions to independence or democratic government, humanitarian relief from natural disaster, and the prevention and mitigation of civil wars or political chaos, would invite many different kinds of UN activity.

For these, in addition to traditional peacekeeping or peace enforcement, greater capacities for preventive diplomacy, peacemaking, and peace-building would be needed. Peace would require the integration of UN institutions directed toward traditional forms of security from military violence with those parts of the United Nations concerned with security from poverty and disease and also with those concerned with the security of political and cultural rights. These other parts of the UN could be used more effectively to prevent some forms of violent conflict from emerging, could inhibit or halt the escalation of violence, and could be brought together to rebuild shattered societies and economies after the violence was over. Seeing these needs and possibilities, he continually expanded our conceptions of the UN's role in international peace and security before those conceptions became common in public discourse.

Operating in part from New Haven, Sutterlin's activities rapidly expanded. He continued to organize conferences—spotting good topics, identifying participants, raising the funding. He and our colleague Jean Krasno conducted an oral history of the United Nations, based on interviews with some of its founders and many UN officers and national policymakers. With Krasno, he recently expanded the project to incorporate an oral history of UNSCOM: the UN's experiences in trying to enforce sanctions and arms inspections on Iraq after the Gulf War. All these materials are now on deposit with the Sterling Library at Yale, the Dag Hammarskjöld Library of the UN in New York, the Soka University of America in Aliso Viejo, California, and Chuo University in Tokyo, Japan. The project on UNSCOM has just become a book, *The United Nations and Iraq: Defanging the Viper,* published by Greenwood/Praeger.

Another of his major projects was to assist Pérez de Cuéllar in the preparation of his memoirs, drawing on documents and his own experience. That book, *Pilgrimage for Peace*, was published in 1997 by St.

Martin's Press. We at Yale all benefited when he brought the secretary-general to the school for a public address and private conversation.

He continued to be an intellectual catalyst for new ideas and perspectives, and as a special adviser contributed heavily to the first draft of Secretary-General Boutros Boutros-Ghali's *Agenda for Peace*. His contribution to the new public discourse on international security was recognized when he was named chairman of the Academic Council in the United Nations System, an organization of scholars and policy intellectuals.

As Sutterlin began to teach at Yale, his seminar restored the study of the UN to our undergraduate curriculum, and he and I taught the first graduate seminar on the United Nations offered here after a lapse of more than a decade. Since then he has regularly taught that course at the graduate and undergraduate levels, and twice since I have had the privilege of coteaching with him what has remained an extremely popular offering.

Subsequently he was wise counselor to Paul Kennedy and me as we served as codirectors of the Secretariat for the 1995 report of the Independent Working Group, *The United Nations in Its Second Half-Century*, under the sponsorship of the Ford Foundation. He also collaborated closely with me in a separate project on options for restructuring the Security Council, which St. Martin's Press published in 1997 as *The Once and Future Security Council*. We benefited as much from his energy as from his intellect. There were nights when a small group of us worked until the morning hours drafting and redrafting passages for the Ford report. Sutterlin might nod a bit early in the evening, but he would quickly spring fully to life and then keep the rest of us going well past the time when our graduate student assistants were fading. We nicknamed him the Energizer Bunny. He remains our regular collaborator in the role of distinguished fellow of the program in United Nations Studies at Yale. There would have been no such program without him, and it is rich for his continued involvement.

This new edition of his book has been thoroughly rewritten, updated, and expanded. It contains a new chapter on terrorism and weapons of mass destruction and new sections on the UN experiences in Kosovo, East Timor, and Sierra Leone. The comprehensiveness of the book illustrates the comprehensiveness of Jim Sutterlin's view. As a senior officer in the United States Foreign Service he developed an appreciation of his country's interest, and as an international civil servant he demonstrated how that interest could be maintained yet transcended. His commitment to a wide and long-term perspective on the national interest and his normative commitment to an inclusive human interest will both be evident to the reader. I am grateful for the gift of providence that brought him to this understanding, that brought him to our intellectual community at Yale, and that continues to bring his wisdom to the global community.

Bruce Russett
Dean Acheson Professor of International Relations
Yale University

Chapter 1

OLD PRINCIPLES, NEW REALITIES

For millennia humans have sought formulas for the maintenance of their security and the peaceful settlement of their conflicts. Each historic era has witnessed the emergence of new ideas—or the reemergence of old— in the hope that the mistakes of the past would not be repeated. With the end of the cold war the world entered again such a period of questioning and exploration.

A NEW PARADIGM

The paradigm of international relations has changed so significantly that it is fair to say that a new era has begun, one which offers hope, but no certainty, that the failed dreams of the past can be realized. A rare, and still fragile, unanimity has been evident that this new era demands a multilateral approach to the resolution of its problems, some inherited from the past, some born in the chaos of adjustment to new conditions of wider freedom, of hatreds rekindled, of the spread of weapons of mass destruction, and of growing challenges to the habitat required for human security.

The United Nations has come to the fore as the lead instrument of choice for most countries to bring peace and productive change. With its new prominence has come proof of enhanced effectiveness and unprecedented responsibilities along with evidence of imperfections and unpreparedness. The United Nations, after all, was born for a different era, the inheritor of many of the norms and a portion of the structure of an organization, the League of Nations, that had failed. To what extent is this organization, more than half a century after its founding, competent to provide security for a new generation of humanity? Where did the concepts that have determined its history originate? How has the United Nations adapted to a changed world, and how can it be further strengthened? Are the purposes and principles on which it was founded relevant and adequate for the realities of this new era? These are the questions with which the present book is concerned.

PRINCIPLES OF THE PAST

Not until the League of Nations was established at the end of the First World War was a structure formed in which the majority of the nations of the world were joined in a commonly accepted responsibility for the maintenance of world peace—not peace within a certain region as had been the case in the Concert of Europe, but peace among all countries. The members of the League were joined, too, in norms of international behavior defined in the League Covenant and in the commitment to take common action, including the automatic application of sanctions, against any "covenant-breaking" country. Thus, for the first time, norms and structure with universal application were combined in a multilateral organization that had for its principal purpose the maintenance of peace.

Central to the potential effectiveness of this organization was the concept of collective security, which is, in essence, the simple principle that all countries will undertake common action against any country that threatens the security of another state—simple in concept, but extraordinarily difficult in practice. The United Nations took over these ideas as its own; it assumed the same global responsibility for the maintenance of international peace and security even though its founders were fully aware that the League had failed. The U.S. undersecretary of state, Sumner Welles, declared already in 1941 that the League "had never been able, as intended, to bring about peaceful and equitable adjustments between nations. . . . Some adequate instrumentality must unquestionably be found to achieve such adjustments when the nations of the earth again undertake the task of restoring law and order to a disastrously shaken world."[1]

A year later, Secretary of State Cordell Hull declared in a radio address that "it is plain to see that some international agency must be created which can—by force, if necessary—keep the peace among nations in the future. There must be international cooperative action to set up the mechanisms that can thus ensure peace."[2] The problem was to avoid those mistakes and inadequacies that had prevented the League from achieving this goal. There were a good many reasons for the League's failure (it had successes as well), but the most important in terms of multilateral effectiveness today were (1) the failure of important states to comply with the provisions of the Covenant; (2) the absence from the League of major states (the United States never joined, the Soviet Union joined late and was subsequently expelled when it invaded Finland, and Germany, Japan, and Italy all withdrew); (3) the ineffectiveness of the means of enforcement action against covenant-breaking states; and, closely related, (4) the readiness of governments, in particular the permanent members of the Council, to place perceived national interests above the common interest of the world community as represented by the League.

STRENGTHENING THE PRINCIPLES OF THE LEAGUE

To overcome these weaknesses, the capacity of the new organization to enforce action against aggression and threats to peace needed to be stronger. With this objective, the unconditional provision was included that all Member States would accept and carry out the decisions of the Security Council (Article 25 of the United Nations Charter). Further, "in order to contribute to the maintenance of international peace and security," members would undertake to make available to the Security Council armed forces, assistance, and facilities, in accordance with special agreements to be completed with each member, to be used by the council to maintain or restore international security. Members were to hold immediately available national air force contingents for combined international enforcement action. A Military Staff Committee was established to advise and assist the Security Council on all questions relating to military requirements for the maintenance of international peace and security and the employment and command of forces placed at its disposal.[3] Thus Member States were clearly committed to accept and carry out the decisions of the Security Council, which would act on behalf of the members in the maintenance of international peace and security. The members would provide the necessary troops and logistic support for the council to do this.[4]

The second cause of the failure of the League of Nations that had to be overcome was the nonparticipation of major countries, especially the United States. To gain the approval of the U.S. Senate, the prerequisite for U.S. membership, it had to be clearly established that action could not be taken to maintain international security that might engage the United States in enforcement action without the concurrence of the U.S. government. For this reason, the U.S. plan for the United Nations provided that the Security Council would have primary responsibility for the maintenance of international security and that only the decisions of the council would be binding on Member States. Any such decisions, except on procedural matters, would require the affirmative vote of the five Permanent Members of the council, the Permanent Members being China, France, the United Kingdom, the Soviet Union, and the United States. In other words, a Permanent Member could veto any action proposed in the council that it perceived as contrary to its interests unless it was a party to the dispute and enforcement action was not involved.[5]

Two central features of the League of Nations were taken over intact. The United Nations was to be an organization of sovereign states without any aspects of supranationality, and it would have no authority to intervene in the domestic affairs of Member States.

One concept of enormous importance was added that distinguished the UN from the League—the concept that satisfaction of the economic, cultural, and humanitarian needs of the global population was an essential element in the maintenance of peace between states. The UN Charter speaks in this context of the objectives of social progress, especially respect for human rights, and better standards of life in larger freedom. U.S. Secretary of State Edward Stettinius in his final report on the Charter to President Harry Truman put it succinctly: "The battle of peace has to be fought on two fronts. The first is the security front where victory spells freedom from fear. The second is the economic and social front where victory means freedom from want."[6] During its first fifty years the dominant portion of the UN's resources was to be devoted to this "second front." However, to a large extent, economic and social development came to be seen as objectives in themselves separate from the UN's primary objective of the maintenance of international security. Now, as the definition of international security has broadened to encompass not only peace between states but also the security of populations within states, economic and social progress are increasingly seen again as essential to international security and peace. The realization, or nonrealization, of these original principles on which the United Nations was based, their observance, or non-observance, and now, increasingly, their interpretation, will define the capacity of the United Nations to deal with the threat and the reality of conflict in the changed circumstances of the twenty-first century.

CAN PAST WEAKNESSES BE OVERCOME?

The United Nations, despite these well-considered principles and concepts, was not, for most of its history, very effective in realizing the security objectives of the Charter. The protection afforded the Permanent Members by the right of veto during this period surely was instrumental in their remaining in the United Nations even when their positions were under severe attack. Now that the Permanent Members of the Security Council have cooperated effectively in the interest of preserving peace, we can see how important it was that they remain in the organization even if they occasionally revert to disunity as in the case of the 2003 war against Iraq. This marks a very positive contrast with the experience of the League of Nations and can be seen as a persuasive justification for the much maligned veto. But this was hardly apparent in the long years during which the Security Council was paralyzed by the cold war. The sad lesson of those years is that a system of collective security that is heavily dependent on decisions to be taken by the Security Council and, *in extremis,* militarily enforced by the council, cannot work effectively unless the Permanent Members are in agreement. For most of the first forty years of the history of the United Nations they were not. The agreements with Member States on the provision of troops and facilities for use by the Security Council provided for in Article 43 of the UN Charter were never reached in large part because of disagreement between the United States and the Soviet Union on the structure and mission such a force would have. Even those decisions that were reached by the council were frequently ignored by Member States. Conflicts were numerous and widespread. As a partial answer, the United Nations developed the technique of peacekeeping; but this was intended to control a conflict situation after, rather than before, conflict had occurred.

It appeared that, apart from retaining all the principal members in the organization, the changes introduced in the United Nations had not made it much more effective in maintaining peace than the League had been. By 1982 Secretary-General Javier Pérez de Cuéllar warned in his first annual report to the General Assembly that ". . . the Council seems powerless. . . . The process of peaceful settlement of disputes prescribed in the Charter is often brushed aside. . . . Sterner measures for world peace were envisaged in Chapter VII of the Charter, which was conceived as a key element of the United Nations system of collective security, but the prospect of realizing such measures is now deemed almost impossible in our divided international community. We are perilously near to a new international anarchy."[7]

The secretary-general was right in his immediate assessment. What he overlooked was that the provisions of the Charter for the maintenance of international security that had proved so ineffective during the arid years of the cold war could and would become effective, at least for a while, once the cold war ended. The application of military force to preserve peace and prevent massive violations of human rights became possible, the injunction against intervention in the domestic affairs of states became subject to reinterpretation, and the United Nations became engaged in the complex undertaking of peace-building. This new potential of the United Nations, as seen in the use of enforcement measures, the undertaking of peace operations, including peace-building, the heightened role of the secretary-general, enhanced cooperation with regional organizations (especially NATO), and the ways in which this potential can be realized, are themes in each of the chapters of this book.

A TIME OF PROGRESS

The years since 1987 have seen significant accomplishments in all of these areas. After the advent to power in the Soviet Union of Mikhail Gorbachev the prospects for an effective Security Council changed significantly. With his policy of conciliation with the West, of "de-ideologizing relations among states"[8] and of strong support for the United Nations, Gorbachev opened the possibility for cooperation among the Permanent Members of the council in dealing with regional conflicts and disputes. Recognizing the importance of this possibility, Secretary-General Pérez de Cuéllar brought the representatives of the five Permanent Members together in March 1987 and called for their joint efforts to end the war between Iraq and Iran, which at that point threatened to spread and directly involve the United States and the Soviet Union. The five cooperated and, with the quiet encouragement and assistance of the secretary-general, together developed the elements for a cease-fire between the two countries that were incorporated in a Security Council resolution on the basis of which the war was finally ended. This collaboration among the Permanent Members, while not widely noted at the time, marked the beginning of a new era for the United Nations.

The agreement on the terms for the cease-fire between Iran and Iraq was followed in quick succession by agreements in the Security Council on the UN plan for Namibia's transition to independence, on the UN's political and military role in the Central American peace process, on the ambitious plan for bringing peace and stability to Cambodia, and in 1990 by the historic decision to repel Iraq's invasion of Kuwait by force. In the case of Central America, the United States made a notable change in its long-standing policy by agreeing to a peace plan in the implementation of which the United Nations would have the central role. The United States had never been willing to rely on the United Nations—or, indeed, to see the United Nations very deeply involved—in Central America or the Caribbean as long as it saw this area as one where the Soviet Union was seeking to expand its influence and was convinced that communism posed a threat to the hemisphere. This change could hardly have happened without the "de-ideologization of international relations" of which Gorbachev spoke.

The positive influence of the end of the cold war on the effectiveness of the Security Council went beyond the achievement of agreement on council resolutions. Because the United States and the Soviet Union were no longer in the position of rival sponsors of countries or internal elements involved in conflict, their influence could be applied on a national basis in tandem with the multilateral decisions of the council in order to encourage implementation of council decisions. The commonality of interests that developed between the great powers in the prevention and resolution of regional conflicts placed them finally on the side of realization of the basic objective of the United Nations. In the new international circumstances the United Sates could recognize that a UN-brokered peace in Central America served the national interests of the United States just as the Soviet Union could see that the UN umbrella provided for the withdrawal of Soviet forces from Afghanistan served its national interests as well as those of the United States.

NEW CHALLENGES

The new coincidence of the interests of the five Permanent Members of the Security Council and the accordance of these interests with the objectives of the UN Charter were hopeful harbingers of what both U.S. president George H. W. Bush and Soviet president Gorbachev referred to as a new world order. But it was soon apparent that the new world order had some highly problematic aspects. Most significantly, the nature of the threats to peace and of conflict assumed characteristics for which the founders of the UN had not planned and with which the UN was not well prepared to deal. The Charter of the United Nations was drafted in the expectation that the Security Council would act to prevent, or to stop, interstate war—wars fought between national armies, across national boundaries. When the Security Council finally gained the extent of agreement among its Permanent Members needed to act effectively against such events, most conflicts in the world stemmed from societal roots rather than rivalry between states and were essentially internal—*intra-state*—in nature. Iraq's invasion of Kuwait was, of course, the old-fashioned kind of war, a vivid indication that this type of threat to the peace cannot be ruled out in the future. But aside from the Gulf War, the conflict situations with which the council has sought to deal in the post–cold war era have been essentially intrastate in nature, albeit with implications going far beyond national borders.

The Central American peace process required not peace between states but peace between warring factions within Nicaragua and El Salvador. In Cambodia, the UN plan to restore stability and freedom entailed su-pervision of civil administration, the resettlement of refugees, and the disarmament of the various armed forces operating in the country. The complexity of the problem of maintaining international security in the post–cold war world was tragically illustrated by the conflict that broke out in what had been Yugoslavia. There, latent nationalism within the federated republics of Slovenia and Croatia, combined with hostility and distrust between the ethnic societies within Yugoslavia, caused Slovenia and Croatia to declare their independence, to be followed shortly there-after by Bosnia and Herzegovina and Macedonia. The nature of the en-suing armed conflict and the UN's involvement will be examined in some detail in a later chapter. It suffices here to note that the United Nations found it necessary, in the interest of peace and the provision of human-itarian assistance, to perform peacekeeping functions between factions within a (newly declared) state; peacemaking functions to bring a solu-tion between the new states; protective functions, within conditions of civil war, to bring humanitarian assistance to the needy population; and all of this in cooperation with the regional organizations that were in-volved in the peace efforts.

The United Nations, even in the new conditions of harmony among the Permanent Members of the Security Council, was not prepared to meet all the new demands that this situation imposed, a situation partially replicated in several of the former republics of the Soviet Union. Other conflicts followed—in Somalia, Haiti, Angola, Rwanda, Sierra Leone, Kosovo, East Timor—that highlighted the manifold questions that arise when the UN undertakes to bring an end to an infringement of basic human rights so massive as to constitute a threat to international security. The Gulf War illustrated the inability of the Security Council to field a UN fighting force under UN command to repel aggression by a major national army. The chaotic conflict in Somalia illustrated the opposite problem, of the inadequacy of the command and control capacity of the

United Nations successfully to carry out an internal enforcement action even when it was able to deploy a significant military force.

Other difficult questions arose as the Security Council and the secretary-general struggled to deal with the new problems that arose one after another in these conflicts. What are the criteria for intervention? What policy should the UN follow if one of the parties to a conflict that had given consent to UN intervention takes hostile action against UN forces (as happened in Somalia)? Are sanctions a proper means of enforcement if great hardship results for the innocent civilian population (as in Iraq)?

In the face of these dilemmas, the newly effective Security Council seemed at times to lose its sense of direction. The problem that had proved fatal to the League of Nations—that is the unwillingness of the major powers to subordinate their national interests to the wider interests represented by the League Covenant—again arose when the United States declared that it would not participate in peacekeeping or peace enforcement actions unless it could be clearly shown that participation was in its own national interest. China vetoed the extension of the preventive peacekeeping deployment along the Macedonia border because Macedonia had established relations with Taiwan. Russia in 2001, mindful of its interest in friendly bilateral relations with Iraq, refused to go along in the Security Council with the introduction of a new and more flexible system of "smart" sanctions because Iraq objected to them. In 2003 the United States and the United Kingdom undertook a war against Iraq without the specific authorization of the Security Council and against the will of most of its members.

DEFINING NEW RULES OF THE GAME

The Security Council recognized that a rethinking of old rules and guidelines and the development of new approaches were needed to take full advantage for peace of the opportunities that a new era in international relations offered. Meeting in January 1991 for the first time in its history at the level of heads of state and government, the council issued a statement noting that the ending of the cold war "has raised hopes for a safer, more equitable and more humane world." After reaffirming the commitment of council members "to the collective security system of the Charter to deal with threats to peace and to reverse acts of aggression," the council invited the secretary-general to provide "his analysis and recommendations on ways of strengthening and making more efficient within the framework and provisions of the Charter the capacity of the United Nations for preventive diplomacy, for peacemaking and for peace-keeping."[9]

Secretary-General Boutros Boutros-Ghali responded in a wide-ranging report entitled *An Agenda for Peace*. Many of the recommendations that he put forward will be considered in the relevant chapters of this book. In the introduction, he reminded all Member States that "the search for improved mechanisms and techniques will be of little significance unless this new spirit of commonality is propelled by the will to take the hard decisions demanded by this time of opportunity."[10] Many involve problems that have been, and remain, hard to resolve. Some, such as redefining the limits of sovereignty, touch on questions that do not lend themselves to clearly defined answers. Under the leadership of Secretary-General Kofi Annan, progress has been made in achieving better system-wide coordination of peace-building and conflict prevention programs. Still, performance is far from perfect. The unilateral trend in the policies of the United States, especially marked since 2001, can adversely affect UN operations and UN authority. Still, the present constellation of international relations, despite these problems, remains the most fortuitous for enhanced effectiveness that the United Nations has enjoyed. It affords an opportunity to adapt and apply the sound principles on which the United Nations was founded to the vastly altered circumstances of a changed world. This is the recurrent theme of the ensuing chapters in which examination is made of the capacity and potential of United Nations to maintain international peace and security.

NOTES

1. Cited in Ruth B. Russell, *A History of the United Nations Charter* (Washington, D.C.: Brookings Institution, 1958), p. 32.

2. Ibid.

3. United Nations Charter, Chapter VII, Articles 42, 43, 45, 47.

4. United Nations Charter, Chapter V, Articles 24, 25.

5. In practice this provision, as incorporated in Article 27 of the UN Charter, has been interpreted to mean that only a negative vote by a Permanent Member constitutes a veto. A resolution may be adopted if one or more Permanent Members abstain or are absent.

6. Edward R. Stettinius, Jr., *Report to the President on the San Francisco Conference,* U.S. Department of State, 26 June 1945.

7. Javier Pérez de Cuéllar, *Anarchy or Order* (New York: United Nations, 1991), p. 6.

8. See the speech of Mikhail Gorbachev to the UN General Assembly on 7 December 1988, printed in the *New York Times*, 8 December 1988.

9. General Assembly document S/23500, 31 January 1992.

10. Boutros Boutros-Ghali, *An Agenda for Peace* (New York: United Nations, 1995).

Chapter 2

PREVENTING CONFLICT

It is often said that it is easier to prevent war than to deal with its consequences. This, unfortunately, is difficult to prove. Successes are hard to confirm, whereas every war and conflict is evidence of failure. Because there have been so many armed conflicts, widely spread through many regions, in the past half-century, one can only conclude that the effectiveness of the United Nations in preventing conflict—a major purpose for which it was created—needs at the very least enhancement. The United Nations has, in reality, been singularly unsuccessful in taking the preventive steps that might arrest a conflict before it reaches the level of armed exchange.

Successive secretaries-general have called for improvement in the preventive diplomacy capacity of the organization. In his 1989 *Report to the General Assembly on the Work of the Organization,*[1] Javier Pérez de Cuéllar wrote the following:

> The prevention of armed conflicts is a mandate envisaged in the provisions of the Charter relating both to the Security Council and the responsibilities of the Secretary-General. Article 34 speaks of any situation which might lead to international friction or give rise to a dispute and Article 99 of any matter which, in the Secretary-General's opinion, may threaten the maintenance of international peace and security. However, as has been repeatedly observed, it has been the general practice over the years to address a particular situation only after it has clearly taken a turn toward the use of force.

One of the three things on which the 1992 Summit Meeting of the Security Council requested the analysis and suggestions of the secretary-general was means of enhancing the effectiveness of the United Nations in preventive diplomacy.

Why has the United Nations been largely unsuccessful until now in this function? How can its performance be improved? To cite a tragic example, why didn't, or couldn't, the United Nations prevent the fratricidal war from breaking out in Bosnia, the genocide in Rwanda, the civil wars in Liberia and Sierra Leone? The answers, to the extent they exist, derive first from the nature of conflict that is to be anticipated and second from the diplomatic tools and the degree of authority available to the United Nations in the given circumstances.

THE NEED FOR PREVENTIVE MEASURES

Conflict between any of the Permanent Members of the Security Council, or between major industrial powers, which inevitably would take on global dimensions, was a terrible nightmare but never a likely reality even during the cold war. Now it is highly improbable. It can be reasonably assumed that in the future, even as now, the conflicts that the United Nations should be in a position to prevent will be regional and, in this geographic sense, limited in nature. They may stem from interstate disputes (as, for example, between India and Pakistan over Kashmir) or between two African countries (because of colonial-era borders). More, however, are likely to stem from societal tensions *within* countries or subregions or from organized terrorism, which has both internal and international consequences. The United Nations must be in a position to take preventive measures against all potential conflicts that can threaten international security.

Dealing with possible internal conflict is something for which no guidelines exist in the UN Charter. The most relevant provision is Article 2, paragraph 7, which states that "Nothing contained in the present Charter shall authorize the United Nations to intervene in matters which are essentially within the domestic jurisdiction of any state. . . ." This is obviously restrictive rather than enabling. Any measures to prevent *intrastate* conflict have to be planned and undertaken with this provision much in mind. Yet if conflicts continue to be predominantly internal in nature, the United Nations cannot meet its mandate to preserve peace without dealing with such conflicts—without seeking in every appropriate way to prevent or mitigate social tensions, deriving from such factors as ethnic or religious division or human rights violations, from escalating to armed violence. Preventive diplomacy, as a result, needs to take forms, such as the resettlement of populations or the training of police forces, that normally would be considered outside of the scope of diplomacy. For this reason *preventive action* is a more accurate term for what is needed to avoid conflict today than *preventive diplomacy*.

Secretary-General Kofi Annan submitted a comprehensive report on conflict prevention to both the General Assembly and the Security Council in June 2001.[2] In his words, "one of the principal aims of preventive action should be to address the deep-rooted socio-economic, cultural, environmental, institutional and other structural causes that often underlie the immediate political symptoms of conflicts."

INFORMATION AND ANALYSIS

There are certain requirements that apply in general to the prevention of conflict whether it be interstate or intrastate in nature. The first is timely information and perceptive analysis. It is patently impossible to prevent something if there is no knowledge that it might happen or inadequate understanding of its causes and possible cures. The United Nations does not have, and is not likely to have, an intelligence operation because governments do not relish being spied on by their own organization. The United Nations is therefore dependent on information provided by governments (often to the secretary-general); on the world media; on academic and institutional sources; on incoming information from UN field posts (a minor source until now except in countries where peacekeeping operations are under way); and on official government declarations, statements, and statistics. These sources if they are well exploited and analyzed can in many cases provide an early indication of regional tension and its causes. However, the capacity of the United Nations Secretariat to assimilate and analyze available information and get it to the secretary-general or the Security Council for action has been inadequate. Moreover, vital intelligence information of a classified nature has frequently not been available to the United Nations.

Two examples may serve to illustrate the past inadequacy of the early warning system, first, in terms of alert analysis, and, second, in terms of the nonavailability of crucial information.

The dispute between Argentina and the United Kingdom over the Falkland Islands had been before the United Nations for many years before Argentina invaded the Falklands on March 31, 1982. The positions of the two countries were fully documented in the records of the General Assembly's Decolonization Committee. Moreover, the two governments had held bilateral talks on their dispute in New York, the last session of which adjourned at the end of February 1982. A communiqué was issued stating that the talks had taken place in a cordial and positive spirit. The resolve of both sides to find a solution to the sovereignty issue was reaffirmed. There appeared no cause, then, for concern. But on March 1, the Argentine Foreign Ministry put out a statement indicating that unless there was an early solution Argentina would choose freely "the procedure that best accorded with its interest." While this was an official, public statement, it was not reported by the UN Information Center in Buenos Aires and it was not noted in the UN Secretariat in New York. At almost the same time, a scrap-metal merchant arrived on South Georgia Island (which was administered by the United Kingdom as a dependency of the Falklands) aboard an Argentine naval vessel and promptly raised the Argentine flag. London reacted sharply, claiming that the scrap-metal workers were illegally occupying British territory, and it sent its sole naval vessel in the area, with twenty-four marines aboard, to remove the scrap-metal workers. Meanwhile, Argentina withdrew most of the workers but sent another naval vessel with a detachment of marines to protect those who had been left on the island. At this point, there were public reports that Argentina was assembling a task force to invade the Falkland Islands.

The developments on South Georgia Island were widely reported in the press and were known in the UN Secretariat. However, there was no office in the Secretariat responsible for following and analyzing such developments in the context of the previous history of the problem and the political environment in the two countries involved. No one in the Secretariat raised a warning flag. Not having been alerted, Secretary-General Pérez de Cuéllar, who was in Europe at the time, did not use his good offices with the parties to try to prevent a conflict or bring the matter to the attention of the Security Council as a potential threat to peace and security. The secretary-general, being from Peru, would have been in a position to communicate effectively with the Argentine leadership. Senior Argentine and British representatives who were in influential positions at the time have indicated that in the face of a warning from the Security Council both countries would have drawn back from confrontation and Argentina would not have gone ahead with the invasion.[3] This conclusion is bound to be speculative, but it does indicate the need for timely information and, equally important, for acute analysis in the UN Secretariat on developments that can lead to war.

The Iraqi invasion of Kuwait in August 1990 provides an illustration of the problem that can arise from a lack of access to crucial information.

Secretary-General Pérez de Cuéllar was aware in mid-summer 1990 of growing tension between Iraq and Kuwait. He knew that Iraq had moved some troops toward the Kuwaiti border. He did not know, however, of the magnitude of the troop movements and therefore had no reason to anticipate an early invasion. Well-informed Arab contacts told him this was highly unlikely.

Both the United States and the Soviet Union knew from satellite photography the size of the Iraqi build-up, but they did not raise the situation in the Security Council nor did they inform the secretary-general. Pérez de Cuéllar has stated that if he had had this information he would have gone to the Security Council, as he is authorized to do under Article 99 of the Charter, in order to warn of a threat to peace. He believes, on the basis of the extensive conversations he had subsequently with Saddam Hussein and the Iraqi deputy prime minister, Tariq Assiz, that Hussein had concluded from his experience when Iraq invaded Iran that the Security Council would in the case of Kuwait again take no early action. This was not an illogical conclusion on his part. Even a public warning from the council, or the dispatch of a small UN fact-finding mission might, in the view of Pérez de Cuéllar, have been sufficient to disillusion Hussein of this conclusion and persuade him to think twice, at least, before proceeding.[4]

This, too, is entirely speculative but the point is nonetheless persuasive. The secretary-general needs to have access to intelligence information from Member States on developing crises so that he can take whatever preventive action is possible.

Secretary-General Boutros-Ghali called for fuller intelligence information from Member States in *An Agenda for Peace.* While the initial response was relatively positive, severe limitations remain. No structural procedure has been established for the regular provision of sensitive information to the secretary-general or his staff. A number of major countries, including the United States, provided highly classified intelligence to the UN Special Commission (UNSCOM) that was established at the end of the Gulf War to seek out and destroy Iraq's weapons of mass destruction capability. However, distribution of this information was strictly controlled and available only to a limited number of UNSCOM staff members. Confidentiality has always been a problem in the United Nations given the multinational character of the Secretariat. While this concern on the part of the United States and Russia has decreased with the end of the cold war, many countries would be extremely resentful if they learned that the secretary-general was being given intelligence information regarding their internal or external disputes by a third country.

Therefore, such information can only be passed with discretion directly to the secretary-general or to one of his immediate associates, a practice that has now begun but only on an ad hoc basis.

Secretary-General Pérez de Cuéllar took several steps to improve the availability of political information and analysis for preventive diplomacy purposes. He first enlarged the mandate of the then more than sixty UN Information Centers around the world to give responsibility to their directors for the submission of regular reports on political developments relevant to the maintenance of international security. This had very limited success. Because of the sensitivity of the host countries, the reports had to be based entirely on unclassified sources. Moreover, many directors were preoccupied with other duties, and some had no concept of the nature of political reporting.

Subsequently, Pérez de Cuéllar established as part of his staff an Office for Research and the Collection of Information (ORCI) with the specific purpose of enhancing the preventive diplomacy capacity of the United Nations. Its mandate was to collect, organize, and analyze political information received from all available sources, including the academic community with which it was to maintain continuing contact. On this basis, it was to advise the secretary-general of threatening developments. ORCI encountered bureaucratic resistance from other Secretariat departments, which were fearful of encroachment on their territory. Moreover, there was insufficient managerial skill to mold the generally gifted staff into a collegial entity that could provide the secretary-general with the timely counsel that was needed. It served, however, as a valuable and much needed conduit to the international academic community from which considerable value was gained.

Secretary-General Boutros-Ghali, intent on introducing extensive reforms in the Secretariat shortly after assuming his position, decided to eliminate ORCI. At the same time, he recognized the need for information and analysis in preventive diplomacy and peacemaking, and he assigned this function to the newly consolidated Department of Political Affairs. The General Assembly in its response to *An Agenda for Peace* subsequently invited the secretary-general "to strengthen the capacity of the Secretariat for the collection of information and analysis to serve better the early-warning needs of the Organization and, to that end, [encouraged] the Secretary-General to ensure that staff members receive proper training in all aspects of preventive diplomacy, including the collection and analysis of information."[5]

The United Nations Institute for Training and Research in Geneva in cooperation with the International Peace Academy undertook such a training program for selected staff members. Kofi Annan reaffirmed the primary responsibility of the Department of Political Affairs for collection and analysis of information for the purpose of conflict prevention. In describing the role of the secretary-general, he stated that he intended "to enhance the traditional preventive role of the Secretary-General in four ways: first, by increasing the use of United Nations interdisciplinary fact-finding and confidence-building missions to volatile regions; second, by developing regional prevention strategies with our regional partners and appropriate United Nations organs and agencies; third, by establishing an informal network of eminent persons for conflict prevention; and fourth, by improving the capacity and resource base for preventive action in the Secretariat."[6]

THE INFORMATION REQUIREMENTS OF A NEW ERA

Given the prominence of social and economic catalysts in conflict in today's world, information and analyses encompassing only political factors are bound to be inadequate for preventive purposes. Economic and social factors need to be incorporated in assessing both the potential for conflict in a particular region or country and the most effective means of averting it. The UN system does not lack for sources of this type of information. It is represented in practically every country of the world, and field representatives of functional agencies are well informed on local economic and social developments that could lead to conflict or humanitarian crises. A system is needed that would permit advantage to be taken of this source of early warning information, something that has been developed with regard to crop prospects and, to a limited extent, with regard to potential refugee flows.

Social, economic, and political factors need to be synthesized, as Annan has suggested, in assessing the need for preventive action and deciding the appropriate measures to be taken. This is now the responsibility of four senior executive committees established by Annan that bring together senior representatives of all Secretariat departments, programs, and funds (except the Specialized Agencies) to consider and make recommendations to the secretary-general on the "core" missions of the United Nations, including conflict prevention.

LIMITATIONS ON PREVENTIVE ACTION

Information and analyses, no matter how timely and acute, cannot in themselves prevent conflict. This is dependent on consequent action. The secretary-general may, within his political mandate under the Charter, act independently, using his good offices in an effort to alleviate the situation. Secretary-General Annan sent interagency missions to several African countries—the first, to Gambia in 2000—for discussions with government officials, political party leaders, representatives of civil society, and members of the UN country teams. The purpose of such missions is to explore the possibility of UN assistance with a view to prevent threats to peace and security in the country concerned. Integration of the programs of the specialized agencies, especially the financial institutions, still leaves much to be desired and remains a problem for the secretary-general.

The secretary-general may, either informally, or formally under the provisions of Article 99 of the Charter, bring a situation to the attention of the Security Council as a threat to international peace and security. There are, however, limitations on the capacity of the secretary-general, acting independently, and of the Security Council to prevent conflict. The secretary-general has only the power of persuasion. He can recommend but he cannot initiate measures for conflict deterrence such as the deployment of peacekeeping forces that might persuade the parties to resolve their differences peacefully; nor can he threaten enforcement measures under Chapter VII of the Charter. Only the Security Council can take such action. The failures of the past forty years have shown that without authoritative support from the Security Council the prevention of conflict is at best doubtful. There would be good reason, then, for the council to have collectively available to it, on a continuing basis, information on developments that could lead to conflict.

The word *collectively* is important. The Permanent Members and some other countries may be adequately informed through national sources. But smaller countries on the council do not have this advantage. They would, as a rule, be more prepared to vote in favor of preventive action on the basis of information from an independent source. The regular provision of information relevant to the maintenance of international security to the council, with, as appropriate, comments and recommendations of the secretary-general, would serve to alert the council and afford it the opportunity—and impose on it a certain additional obligation—to become involved at an early stage in seeking to prevent conflict. Toward this objective, a system should be developed under which information deemed significant is forwarded to the council on a regular schedule as well as on an ad hoc basis by the secretary-general if a particularly threatening situation needs to be highlighted.

Tentative steps have been taken in this direction by the Secretariat but so far without much impact. The Economic and Social Council (ECOSOC) is required under the Charter to assist the Security Council on the council's request.[7] The Security Council can therefore call on ECOSOC for information and reports on economic and social developments relevant to the maintenance of international security. The council has never until now made such a request. Even should it do so, it will not lessen the need for analysis and advice from the secretary-general in which all factors—political, military, economic, and social—have been taken into account.

The Security Council also has the possibility, as does the secretary-general, of sending a fact-finding mission to an area of tension to seek information on the basis of which the council can decide what preventive action can be taken. In recommending that greater use be made of fact-finding, Secretary-General Boutros-Ghali pointed out in *An Agenda for Peace* that the dispatch of such a mission can, in itself, sometimes serve a preventive purpose by giving a clear indication to the parties of UN concern and by providing a temporary UN presence in the area that can encourage de-escalation of tension.

The Security Council, like the secretary-general, lacks the authority and means to deploy economic and financial resources to alleviate threatening internal tension within countries or regions. In a time when conflict most often derives from social and economic roots, this is a serious inhibition for longer-range preventive action by the United Nations. The availability of adequate economic and financial resources must be seen as an essential, and presently unavailable, tool for conflict prevention. For this reason, some authorities have begun to question the emphasis that Annan and others have placed on dealing with the root causes of conflict and have suggested that priority should be given to the operational means of conflict prevention that are more consonant with the UN's realistic capability.[8]

MEDIATION

A further requirement for success in preventing conflict—after full and timely information acquisition and analysis—is mediation skill. In conflict situations where armed exchange has occurred, the United Nations has shown over the years a commendable mediation capability. This has been seen in the achievement by the secretary-general or his representative of an understanding on the withdrawal of Soviet forces from Afghanistan, the realization of the cease-fire in the Iran-Iraq war, and the negotiation of a settlement of the civil strife in El Salvador. Other instances could be cited of skillful mediation even though the results were not satisfactory. Moreover, reinforcement of the UN's in-house capacity is easily available, as in the enlistment of Olaf Palme in the Iran-Iraq war, Cyrus Vance in the Yugoslav crisis, and James Baker in the Western Sahara conflict. In the past, panels of experts for inquiry and conciliation as well as for fact-finding have been established by the General Assembly.[9] They have almost never been used, but they can be revived at any time. The failures in preventing interstate conflict have not resulted from inadequate mediation means. There is no lack of skilled mediators available to the United Nations.

It needs to be recognized, however, that a different kind of mediation expertise is needed to deal with strife deriving from social tensions within a society. This is an area where the United Nations has only begun to acquire extensive experience in Kosovo, East Timor, and Sierra Leone. Mediation in situations of domestic tension can only be afforded at the invitation of the government or of the parties concerned. But the secretary-general or one of the other organs of the UN can take the initiative in suggesting the utility of third-party mediation or conciliation. The secretary-general could develop a pool of social conciliators (as could regional organizations) and indicate the availability of this service and its merits in resolving a particular situation. As stated earlier, Annan has already sent interagency teams to Africa to explore the possibilities of UN assistance. Secretary-General Pérez de Cuéllar, in the mid-1970s, sent an interagency team to assess what could be done to alleviate a severe famine that threatened the security of sub-Saharan Africa. It must be recognized that governments will not always accept UN assistance and that there will be situations in which the United Nations cannot be helpful, but this should not be interpreted as meaning the approach is not worth pursuing.

LEVERAGE

Leverage can be seen as yet another essential element in preventive diplomacy. No matter how skillful the mediator may be, conflict prevention often requires the application of some form of pressure if it is to succeed. Such leverage, whether in the form of proffered benefits or threatened punishment, is largely dependent on action by the Security Council, the General Assembly, UN functional organizations (for the provision of benefits), or from Member States. One looks first to the Security Council in this connection because it has mandatory power and primary responsibility for the maintenance of peace.

The Security Council cannot impose a solution to an interstate or intra-state dispute either before or after armed conflict occurs. This possibility was debated at the San Francisco Conference in 1945 and intentionally excluded from the council's mandate. However, the council now has means of persuasion—or dissuasion—that during the period of the cold war were practically nonexistent. The great advantage offered by council action derives from the possibility of bringing to bear the *combined* influence of its members, thus intensifying the effect and, of at least equal importance, helping to ensure that the Permanent Members of the council do not find themselves acting to contrary purpose in a given dispute, as was usually the case during the first four decades of the UN's history and again, unfortunately, in the elimination of weapons of mass destruction in Iraq.

Governments, before embarking on an adventuresome policy, must now take into account the real possibility that the Security Council may, if necessary, agree on enforcement measures to maintain international security. The credibility of council action translates into substantial leverage that can be applied for preventive purposes. For this leverage to be sustained, the members of the council, and other Member States on the request of the council, must adjust their national policies toward the parties to a dispute so as to support the objectives agreed on and articulated by the council. Given the leverage that derives from a Security Council recognized as capable of effective action, there is a range of preventive measures that the council can undertake with reasonable hope of success. Among the most important are the following, most of which were suggested by Secretary-General Boutros-Ghali in *An Agenda for Peace:*

Public Warning—A Security Council resolution warning of the danger to peace in a situation, calling on the parties to exercise restraint and making clear that the council will remain seized of the problem, can sometimes have a calming effect. As noted earlier, such action was lacking prior to the Argentine invasion of the Falkland Islands and the Iraqi invasion of Kuwait.

Fact-Finding Missions—The dispatch of a fact-finding team or individual can add to the credibility of a warning resolution and, at the same time, provide a basis for further council action. Such a mission can also serve to halt the process of escalation and provide, like discussion in the Security Council, a cooling-off period for the parties in dispute. Secretary-General Boutros-Ghali sent fact-finding emissaries to several of the new states in the former Soviet Union that faced the possibility of internal conflict, involving in some cases disputes with a neighboring state. The results were favorable, if hardly decisive.

Designation of a Special Representative—The council can call on the secretary-general to extend his good offices or can appoint a special representative to assist the parties in resolving their dispute. This would not, in principle, require the prior consent of the parties, but their co-operation would obviously be essential.

Referral to the International Court of Justice—In conjunction with one or all of the above measures, the council can, in an interstate dispute, urge the parties to refer their dispute to the International Court of Justice for adjudication. Several secretaries-general have requested that the General Assembly grant them similar authority, but the assembly has never complied.

Establishment of Demilitarized Zones—In instances of tension and distrust between neighboring states, the council can suggest, as a confidence-building measure, the establishment of demilitarized areas along both sides of the border. If the parties agree, the council can dispatch an observer mission to monitor the area to give further assurance to both parties against surprise attack. If such action is taken in conjunction with the designation of a special representative, it can improve the atmosphere for the latter's mediation efforts.

Provision of Humanitarian and Economic Assistance—If peace is threatened by an internal dispute that derives from economic or social causes, the council should be able to call on the secretary-general to mobilize resources from the UN system (and possibly from Member States) that can be quickly applied to alleviate the situation. This would be a new departure for the council, constituting a form of peace-building for preventive purposes. This subject is discussed in greater detail in chapter 5 of this book.

These measures have been described in terms of the secretary-general and the Security Council. This is not intended to exclude the General Assembly as a source of leverage in preventing conflict. The assembly can, if it is in session, adopt appropriate warning resolutions and call on the parties to refer their dispute to the International Court of Justice, thus mobilizing public opinion and government support in behalf of a peaceful resolution.[10] If, in a situation of internal tension, assistance is needed in organizing an election or monitoring the vote, the assembly is the logical body to call on the secretary-general to provide it. The special office in the Secretariat to give such assistance was established at the assembly's request. In assessing the prospect of preventive action by the General Assembly, however, it is well to keep in mind that the end of the cold war did not alter the orientation of the assembly to the same extent that it did that of the Security Council. Elimination of the division between East and West did little to lessen the division between North and South. Dominated, as it is, by Third World countries, many members of the assembly are concerned lest UN preventive action infringe on the sovereignty of a small country. The assembly can therefore be expected to act with caution, if at all, in calling for preventive measures in the case of internal conflict or in pressing a Member State to accept them. The relationship between the Security Council and the General Assembly in dealing with threats of internal conflict or humanitarian crises is sensitive and still in need of definition.

INSTRUMENTS FOR DETERRENCE

Another element that can be important in the prevention of conflict is the availability of a *deterrence instrumentality*. The United Nations has such an instrumentality in the form of peacekeeping forces (including military observer missions) that can be deployed to decrease the likelihood of both interstate and intrastate conflict. A peacekeeping force was deployed for the first time for strictly deterrent purposes in Macedonia at the beginning of 1993 but this action has, so far, not been repeated elsewhere. This subject is pursued further in the immediately following chapters on the use of military force.

WHY PREVENTION CAN FAIL

The cooperative relationship that developed among the Permanent Members of the Security Council, particularly between Russia and the United States, as the cold war came to an end unquestionably enhanced the potential of the United Nations in the prevention of conflict. The mere fact that there was no division between East and West—that in a given dispute the United States was not on one side and the Soviet Union on the other—added to the influence, or leverage, that the council could exert. Unity in the council also increased the credibility of the secretary-general as a peacemaker. Yet the United Nations was not able to prevent the deplorable conflicts in the former Yugoslavia, Rwanda, East Timor, Ethiopia/Eritrea, or Sierra Leone. Why not? First of all, several of the requirements of conflict prevention that have been described earlier were not yet in place. There was no effective early warning mechanism in the Secretariat at the time Yugoslavia disintegrated. There was no policy planning staff to explore options for UN action and to examine the ap-

propriate and realistic roles for the UN and the European regional organizations, nor was an effective liaison arrangement between them in
existence. More importantly, the concepts of the utilization of peacekeeping for deterrence and for peace enforcement had not yet been accepted in the United Nations. The organization was unprepared for the
disasters.

When conflict first occurred in Croatia at the time of its declaration
of independence and the Croats and rebellious Serbs reached cease-fires
but did not comply with them, the UN, holding to the traditional concept
of peacekeeping, refused to send peacekeepers to enforce compliance.
When a large peacekeeping force was subsequently deployed in Croatia
after much loss of life and destruction of property, it was given a mandate
that could only be successfully implemented by the application of force
that the peacekeepers were not authorized or equipped to use. Peacekeeping, then, was an insufficiently credible instrumentality to establish
the necessary conditions for lasting peace in Croatia or to deter the subsequent outbreak of war in Bosnia.

Another factor at the time of the dissolution of Yugoslavia was the
untested capability of the regional organizations and the lack of clarity
as to the roles that they and the United Nations could most usefully play.
Pride of place was given first to the regional organizations, which delayed somewhat the focused intervention of the UN.

The Croatian experience offered these lessons to the United Nations,
lessons clearly reflected in the recommendations contained in Boutros-
Ghali's *Agenda for Peace*. Steps have been taken to establish an early
warning mechanism; clarification and enhancement of the relationship
between regional organizations and the UN is being pursued; and the
concepts of the deterrent utilization of peacekeeping and of peace enforcement have become realities. The deployment of peacekeepers to
Macedonia to deter external intervention can be seen as a first fruit of
the combination of the post–cold war consensus in the Security Council
and the availability of new instrumentalities for deterrence.

Having recorded these positive developments that offer hope of greater
UN effectiveness in preventing conflict, it must be added that in the case
of Bosnia, there was advance warning of possible catastrophe, with prescient analysis from the secretary-general's envoy in Yugoslavia. Vance
informed Secretary-General Pérez de Cuéllar that international recognition of Croatia and its admission to the United Nations before a resolution was found for the overall problem of Yugoslavia would inevitably
lead to a declaration of independence by Bosnia and civil war there. The
secretary-general spoke with the Permanent Members of the Security

Council and found that there was no inclination toward precipitate recognition of Croatia. The United States, in particular, shared the secretary-general's view that recognition was undesirable at that point. Realizing that pressure for recognition came from the German government (which was not on the Security Council), Pérez de Cuéllar wrote directly to German foreign minister Hans Dietrich Genscher and, in what for him were unusually brusque terms, warned that recognition of Croatia (and Slovenia) could do incalculable harm. Genscher replied to the effect that this was not the secretary-general's business. Pérez de Cuéllar nonetheless sent a further letter warning against recognition of the two newly declared independent countries. This preventive diplomacy was to no avail. Recognition of Croatia and Slovenia followed quickly under German pressure, as did their admission as full members to the United Nations.

This history is recounted here to illustrate that there can be factors affecting the likelihood of conflict that are outside the capacity of even an invigorated United Nations to control. Nevertheless, given a broad commonality of interests among the Permanent Members of the Security Council (one of which is the prevention or resolution of regional conflict), and the availability of preventive measures newly developed or newly applicable, the United Nations can be a very effective force in preventing conflict. To ensure this, the credibility of the preventive measures must be maintained. Any potential aggressor must be convinced of the UN's capacity to respond. Any disaffected element in a society threatened by social violence must be convinced that the United Nations has access to resources that can alleviate the causes of tension. Forces deployed in the field by the United Nations must be adequately mandated, equipped, and financed to accomplish the objectives expected of them. In the cases of failure cited earlier, one or more of the UN's prevention tools was absent. But in the final analysis, the effectiveness of the United Nations in preventing conflict will be determined most of all by the credibility of the Security Council and the readiness of its members to take action before the outbreak of violent conflict forces them to do so. This is something that the Security Council has been very reluctant to do.

NOTES

1. Javier Pérez de Cuéllar, *Anarchy or Order.* (New York: United Nations, 1991), p. 228.

2. UN document A/55/985-S/2001/574, 7 June 2000.

3. Interviews with Niconor Costa-Mendez and Sir Anthony Parsons, UN Oral History Collection, Yale University Library.

4. Unpublished interview by the author with Javier Pérez de Cuéllar.

5. A/RES/47/120 (1992).

6. UN document A/55/985-S/200/574, 7 June 2001, p. 16.

7. UN Charter, Chapter X, Article 65.

8. See Edward C. Luck, "Prevention: Theory and Practice," in *From Reaction to Conflict Prevention*," ed. Fen Osler Hampson and David M. Malone (Boulder, Colo.: Lynne Rienner, 2002).

9. A description of the various fact-finding and mediation panels established in the past may be found in General Assembly document A/10289, 20 October 1975.

10. The first UN peacekeeping operation, the UN Emergency Force in the Sinai, was authorized in 1956 by the General Assembly, Security Council action having been blocked by British and French vetoes. It is now generally accepted, however, that only the Security Council can authorize the deployment of peacekeeping forces.

Chapter 3

MILITARY FORCE IN THE SERVICE OF PEACE: PEACEKEEPING IN INTRASTATE CONFLICT

To maintain peace by military force may seem at first glance—and even second glance—an oxymoron. The term *peace enforcement* suffers from the same problem. Yet a primary element in the concept of collective security on which the United Nations is based is that military force will be used, if necessary, to maintain peace and international security. As the meaning of international security has broadened, and as conflict has become increasingly intrastate in character, the purposes for which the application of military force may be needed in one form or another have also become more varied. This is amply evidenced by the UN, or UN-authorized, operations in Namibia, Central America, the Persian Gulf, Cambodia, the former Yugoslavia, Somalia, Sierra Leone, East Timor, and elsewhere. In the post–cold war era, the use of military personnel (together frequently with police and civilian personnel) has assumed new dimensions and new potential, owing in large part to the prevalence of intrastate conflict. This has raised many questions both for the United Nations and for its Member States regarding expanded military deployment, in particular the adequacy of resources, the procedures for command and control, and the possible infringement of national sovereignty.

A HISTORY OF DOMESTIC INVOLVEMENT

The purpose of UN peacekeeping forces has traditionally been understood as that of interpositioning, with the consent of the parties concerned, between two hostile forces after a truce or cease-fire has been achieved to discourage a resumption of hostilities. From the beginning, however, the purpose went beyond that. In the first full-fledged UN peacekeeping operation, mounted as a result of the Suez War in 1956, the original purpose was to "secure and supervise the cessation of hostilities in accordance with the aforementioned resolution" (which included the withdrawal of foreign forces from Egyptian territory).[1] This was expanded, or interpreted, in accordance with subsequent General Assembly resolutions, to include deployment in the Gaza Strip to maintain quiet during and after the withdrawal of Israeli forces and to prevent illegal crossings of the armistice line by civilians of either side. Notably, the United Nations Emergency Force (UNEF) was expected to assume responsibility for the civil administration of the Gaza Strip and did so for a brief period until Egypt moved in with its forces.

In the ensuing years, peacekeeping has encompassed such varied functions as to make definition difficult. To appreciate the role that peacekeeping can play in intrastate conflicts, it is useful to examine the ways in which six diverse UN peacekeeping operations were involved in the domestic concerns of the countries where they were deployed: the Congo, Cyprus, southern Lebanon, Namibia, Nicaragua, and Haiti.

THE CONGO

A UN peacekeeping force, the United Nations Operation in the Congo (ONUC), was sent to the Congo essentially to stabilize conditions that had become chaotic and violent when the country gained independence from Belgium. The new government requested UN military assistance "to protect the national territory of the Congo against the present external aggression which is a threat to international peace."[2] There was no request to restore internal stability. However, Secretary-General Dag Hammarskjöld recommended to the Security Council the establishment of a peacekeeping force to assist the government of the Congo in maintaining law and order until, with technical assistance from the United Nations, the Congolese national security forces were able to meet these tasks. The Security Council authorized the secretary-general to take the necessary steps for this purpose and called on Belgium to withdraw its troops from the territory.[3] Thus began what until the operation in Cambodia was the largest UN peacekeeping operation (reaching a peak of 20,000 troops plus a large civilian corps) and one with a profound influence on internal developments in a Member State.[4]

The secretary-general was fully aware of the sensitivity of the action that the United Nations was undertaking in the Congo both in terms of the attitudes of the foreign countries with a strong interest in the course of events in the Congo and the resistance of the Congolese government to any seeming challenge to its authority within the country, even though such authority was highly tenuous. In his first report to the Security Council on the Congo operation, Hammarskjöld stated the principles that would govern the activities of ONUC, among which were the following:

- Although dispatched at the request of the Congolese Government, and although it might be considered as serving as an arm of the Government for the purpose of the maintenance of law and order and protection of life, the Force was necessarily under the exclusive command of the United Nations. The Force is thus not under the orders of the Congolese Government and cannot be permitted *to become a party to any internal conflict.*

- The authority of the United Nations Force may not be exercised within the Congo either in competition with the representatives of its government or in co-operation with them in any joint operation. The United Nations operation must be separate and distinct from activities by any national authorities.

- The Force cannot be used to enforce any specific political solution of pending problems or to influence the political balance decisive for such a solution.

- The United Nations military units are not authorized to use force except in self-defense. They are never to take the initiative in the use of force, but are entitled to respond with force to an attack with arms, including attacks intended to make them withdraw from positions they occupied under orders of the Force Commander.[5]

Each of these principles was severely tested during the Congo operation and, in some instances, rather elastically interpreted. Patrice Lumumba, the first prime minister of the Congo, never understood or accepted that the UN force could not be used in collaboration with Congolese troops to end the secession of Katanga. The failure of Hammarskjöld to use the UN force for this purpose was a major factor in the withdrawal by the Soviet Union of confidence in the secretary-general.

The principle of non-use of force was equally difficult to apply and had eventually to be modified. For one thing, commanders in the field, unused to the subtleties of UN language, did not know how to interpret the principle in practice. In visits to the Congo, the secretary-general's military advisor found the commanders confused. He sought to clarify for them individually how the principle was to be interpreted.[6]

In light of the deteriorating security situation in the Congo, the Security Council on February 21, 1961, adopted a resolution authorizing the use of force, if necessary as a last resort, to prevent civil war there.[7] Hammarskjöld was not entirely happy with this resolution as not providing "a wider legal basis" for action;[8] nonetheless, on the basis of this resolution UN forces took military action in Katanga that contributed decisively to ending its secession and that could be seen as at odds with the principle enunciated earlier by Hammarskjöld (and approved by the Security Council) that the UN force could not be used to enforce any specific political solution of pending problems or become party to any internal conflict.

Simultaneously with efforts to maintain security and law and order in the Congo, the UN force (primarily through its civilian component) undertook to assure the continuation of essential services, to restore and organize the administrative machinery of government, and to train the Congolese to run that machinery.[9] For these purposes UN staff members were placed in the government ministries and in provincial offices as well as in infrastructure operational facilities. Certain police responsibilities were carried out. The representative of the secretary-general even exercised authority over the functioning of the Léopoldville airport and the Léopoldville radio (which was interpreted by some as contrary to the principle of not taking sides in internal conflicts, enunciated by Hammarskjöld).

Although a major concern of Hammarskjöld in recommending UN action in the Congo was the possibility that the situation there could bring the United States and the Soviet Union into direct conflict, the resolution authorizing the deployment of the peacekeeping force makes no reference to the danger that the situation posed to international security. The Security Council called for the withdrawal of Belgian troops, but the objectives established for the peacekeeping force were internal. No reservations were expressed that the action might be contrary to Article 2, paragraph 7, of the UN Charter, possibly because the Belgian military intervention lent a clear international dimension to the crisis. Nonetheless, it can hardly be contested that the Congo operation was undertaken to deal with an intrastate situation. The operation revealed the serious—even fatal—problems that such an operation can entail, especially when undertaken within an environment of hostility and mistrust between the United States and the Soviet Union.

The problems were not only those related to the role of the United Nations in the conflicts between the various Congolese factions and in the Katanga secession. There were also problems that derived from the capability of the United Nations to perform a task of such size and complexity. Given the number of troops required, some inevitably were inadequately trained and prepared for peacekeeping duties. Some senior military officers were incompetent, and some senior civilian personnel showed mistaken judgment. The internal nature of the situation with which the UN was dealing brought the secretary-general under harsh attack, with serious implications for his continued effectiveness in leading the organization had he lived. A financial strain was placed on the United Nations that was to trouble the organization for many years. The attitude of many UN members toward the UN–Congo operation was for many years "never again."

Yet, in the perspective of more than forty years, the UN–Congo operation must be viewed as a success and one with positive implications and prescient warnings for the UN's future involvement in intrastate conflicts. Internal stability was restored; the territorial integrity of a newly decolonized country was maintained; the danger of East-West conflict was avoided; and the United Nations proved its capacity—even if imperfect—to mount a large operation and to carry it through within an environment of domestic violence and, at times, hostility toward the UN itself.

The principles formulated by Hammarskjöld with reference to the Congo were intended to ensure the complete impartiality of the UN peacekeeping force and to avoid any conflict with the provision in the UN Charter prohibiting intervention in the domestic affairs of states. They could hardly be formulated otherwise today. Yet, in practice it now proves even less practical than then to comply strictly with such principles and still achieve an end to internal conflict.

CYPRUS

In the face of the violent conflict that had broken out between the Greek and the Turkish Cypriot communities in Cyprus, the Security Council, at the request of the governments of Cyprus and the United Kingdom, decided in March 1964 that a UN peacekeeping force should be sent to the island. In the resolution that was adopted,[10] it was noted that the situation in Cyprus was likely to endanger international peace and security. But the mandate that was given to the United Nations Peace-keeping Force in Cyprus (UNFICYP) pertained entirely to the intrastate conflict. Specifically the force was to prevent a recurrence of fighting between the communities and to contribute to the maintenance and restoration of law and order and a return to normal conditions. This has remained UNFICYP's core mandate to the present day even though it has had to be exercised under the vastly changed conditions that resulted from the 1974 coup d'état, the subsequent Turkish invasion, and the effective partitioning of the island.

As in the case of the Congo, the secretary-general (at this time U Thant) recommended, and the Security Council approved, notably similar principles that were to guide the activities of UNFICYP,[11] among which were the following:

- The Force must be under the exclusive control and command of the United Nations at all times.
- The Force will undertake no functions inconsistent with the provisions of the Security Council resolution.
- The Force will use arms only for self-defense in the interest of preserving international peace and security, of preventing a recurrence of fighting and of contributing to the maintenance and restoration of law and order and normal conditions.
- The personnel of the Force must act with restraint and complete impartiality towards the Greek and Turkish Cypriot communities.

With the Congo experience no doubt in mind, Secretary-General U Thant, in his report to the Security Council, made a special effort to clarify how "self-defense" was to be interpreted. Self-defense, he said, includes the defense of UN posts, premises, and vehicles under armed attack, as well as the support of other UNFICYP personnel under armed attack. "Examples in which troops may be authorized to use force include attempts by force to compel them to withdraw from a position which they occupy under orders from their commanders, attempts by force to disarm them, and attempts by force to prevent them from carrying out their responsibilities as ordered by their commanders."[12] The self-defense, of course, would be against hostile *domestic* forces under the UNFICYP mandate. A very similar definition of self-defense was applied in the UN peacekeeping operation in Bosnia and Herzegovina.

Given the nature of its mandate "to contribute to the maintenance and restoration of law and order and a return to normal conditions,"[13] UNFICYP was established with a civilian police component (UNCIVPOL). Among the duties defined by the secretary-general for this police force was the investigation of incidents where Greek and Turkish Cypriots were involved with the opposite community, including searches for persons reported as missing. At a later stage, after the Turkish invasion in 1974, it was agreed that UNFICYP would be responsible for all security and police functions in mixed villages.

In fact, both the military and civilian components of UNFICYP have been directly involved in what normally would be considered the functions of the domestic authorities, whether national or municipal. It can hardly be otherwise in any situation in which a UN peacekeeping force has responsibility for preventing a recurrence of conflict and maintaining law and order among hostile elements of a national society. Moreover, restoration of law and order and a return to normal conditions have entailed extensive humanitarian and logistic assistance by UNFICYP. Electric power in the northern part of the island is supplied from the southern part. Water sources flow across the cease-fire lines and sometimes crisscross the buffer zone. Assistance is provided to Greek Cypriots and Maronites in the north and Turkish Cypriots in the south including medical evacuation when needed. After the landing of Turkish troops in 1974, the humanitarian needs were so great that a special humanitarian and economics branch was set up at UNFICYP headquarters. With as many as one-third of the island's population displaced, however, humanitarian needs were beyond the capacity of the peacekeeping operation, and the UN high commissioner for refugees was designated as coordinator of UN humanitarian assistance for Cyprus, thus enlisting a separate UN office in meeting responsibilities assumed by the United Nations as part of peacekeeping.

Since the Turkish invasion, UNFICYP has been, in effect, the administering authority in the buffer zone established between the forces on the two sides in 1974. This covers 3 percent of the island and includes some of its most valuable agricultural land. According to the December 7, 1990, Report of a Secretariat Review Team on the United Nations Peacekeeping Force in Cyprus:

> There is no formal agreement between UNFICYP and the two sides on the complete delineation of the buffer zone. As a result, UNFICYP finds itself supervising, by loose mutual consent, two constantly disputed cease-fire lines. . . . In addition to its constant endeavors to maintain the military *status quo* UNFICYP must also preserve the integrity of the buffer zone from unauthorized entry or activities by civilians. As a result, UNFICYP has become increasingly involved in crowd control. . . . While the primary responsibility for preventing demonstrators from crossing the cease-fire line rests with the civilian authorities concerned, UNFICYP troops and UNCIVPOL . . . must prevent demonstrators from entering the buffer zone.
>
> Farming permits are issued [by UNFICYP] to proven owners of land. . . . To take into account the security requirements of the two sides as well as the safety of the farmers, UNFICYP has drawn up farming

security lines to delimit the farming area within the buffer zone. . . . In areas that have proven to be contentious, farmers from either community are escorted by UNFICYP troops on a daily basis. . . . UNFICYP must keep the farming area under constant supervision from observation posts or through patrols.[14]

If a crime is committed in the buffer zone, it is an open question who has the authority to arrest.

Today, almost forty years after its deployment, UNFICYP is taken for granted by both sides in Cyprus. Back in April 1991 the author had the opportunity to meet with the UNFICYP force commander and members of both his military and civilian staff to observe UNFICYP operations and to talk with senior officials on both the Greek Cypriot and Turkish Cypriot sides. UNFICYP activities that touch on the domestic adminis-tration of the island had not led to any appreciable resentment or resis-tance on the part of local authorities, although the Cyprus government was sensitive to any implied derogation of its territorial sovereignty. The only complaint voiced in the Foreign Ministry of Cyprus pertained to the issuance of passes by UNFICYP for entry to the buffer zone. The ministry took exception to this practice as inappropriate because this was a function of the sovereign government, but this was not portrayed as a serious issue. Interestingly, the only major complaint stated by senior representatives on both the Greek Cypriot and Turkish Cypriot sides was that the United Nations should have from the beginning been more ag-gressive in *enforcing* peace on the island. The peacekeeping operation was viewed in this perspective as misguided and ineffective, although no one suggested that within the limits of its mandate UNFICYP had not been extremely useful, even essential to the security and well being of the island. And, of course, the two sides have sharply conflicting views as to what regime the United Nations should have enforced to bring peace.

UNFICYP has never had a peacemaking mandate. This function rests with the secretary-general and his special representative for Cyprus. It might have been expected, however, that the extensive UNFICYP hu-manitarian activities would have brought some conciliation, at least at the local level, between the two sides. This has not been the case. On one hand, UNFICYP has facilitated the peacemaking process by stabi-lizing the security situation on the island, without which the political efforts to resolve the Cyprus problem—unproductive as they have been— could not have gone forward. The decision by Turkish Cypriot authorities in May 2003 to allow free entry to northern Cyprus by Greek Cypriots was made without consultation or coordination with UNFICYP. However, the step would hardly have been possible had UNFICYP not contributed to the development of a peaceful atmosphere during the long years of its presence in Cyprus.

SOUTHERN LEBANON

The United Nations Interim Force in Lebanon (UNIFIL) was deployed in March 1978 in immediate response to the invasion of southern Lebanon by Israel. To appreciate the responsibilities it was given and the role it plays even today, however, the deployment of the force must be seen in the larger context of the civil war that had engulfed Lebanon in 1975. As a result of that war and the expansion of control by the Palestine Liberation Organization (PLO) in the south, the Lebanese government was unable to exercise its authority south of the Litani River, the area invaded by Israel. Therefore UNIFIL was deployed into an area where the national government did not govern, where a foreign army was in the field, and where a number of local authorities vied for control. It is hardly surprising under the circumstances that the mandate defined for UNIFIL was less than clear. Patently, it would have to operate within a complex domestic environment.

The Security Council, in authorizing the deployment of UNIFIL, stated three purposes for the force:

- confirm the withdrawal of Israeli forces;
- restore international peace and security;
- assist the Lebanese government to restore its authority in the area.

The secretary-general defined, as in previous peacekeeping undertakings, terms of reference for UNIFIL, terms that had to take account of the internal role that was to be played. Among the provisions were the following:

- The force would establish and maintain itself in an "area of operation" to be defined in light of the tasks set by the Security Council.
- It would seek to prevent the recurrence of fighting.
- It would ensure that its area of operation would not be used for hostile activities of any kind.
- Once the withdrawal of Israeli forces from Lebanese territory was confirmed, it would control movement in the area and take all necessary measures to restore the authority of the Lebanese government.[15]

In stating these principles the secretary-general placed particular emphasis on the non-use of force and nonintervention in the internal affairs of the host country. UNIFIL must not take on responsibilities that fell under the government of the country in which it was operating.[16]

It was never possible to agree with the parties concerned on an official definition of the area in which UNIFIL was to operate. As Israeli forces withdrew from southern Lebanon, UNIFIL established itself in the area except in an enclave considered by Israel to be particularly sensitive in terms of PLO infiltration. There a militia under the command of Lebanese major Saad Haddad, termed by the United Nations de facto forces, took over and refused to allow UNIFIL to deploy, thus enormously complicating UNIFIL's task. These forces were supported and directed by Israel, and Israeli military personnel continued to be present in this area, sometimes moving also into the area of UN deployment.

The principles for the operation defined by the secretary-general entailed an inherent contradiction. The UN force was not to take on the responsibilities of the Lebanese government, but in reality the Lebanese government was not able to exercise its authority in the area. The task of assisting the Lebanese government to restore its authority inevitably involved undertaking activities that would normally be the responsibility of the government in Beirut until the government was able to do so.

Looking to the future functioning of UN peacekeeping, it is of some importance to consider what UNIFIL has accomplished given the restrictions in its mandate and the extraordinarily complex circumstances in which it has operated. Taking the purposes defined for it by the Security Council, which despite changing circumstances have not been materially altered, how far has it progressed toward accomplishing them?

The first purpose was to confirm the withdrawal of Israeli forces from Lebanese territory, a traditional function of UN peacekeeping in cases of interstate conflict. But in Lebanon the objective of bringing about the withdrawal of foreign forces assumed an intrastate dimension when the Israeli forces were replaced in important respects by the internal de facto forces eventually called the South Lebanon Army. UNIFIL was neither mandated nor equipped to do battle with this surrogate force, even though the force prevented the full deployment of UNIFIL and at times attacked UNIFIL posts. (The use of force by UNIFIL has never been authorized in southern Lebanon as it was in the Congo.)

The second purpose was restoring international peace and security in the area. International peace and security were and still are affected by violence and conflict in Lebanon. The extensive presence of Syrian forces in the country and the two Israeli invasions, in particular, have given a clear interstate dimension to the conflict. Yet, aside from confirming the withdrawal of Israeli forces, UNIFIL was not in a position to influence the larger *international* factors in the security situation in its area of operation. When the second Israeli invasion occurred, traversing in the process the area of UN deployment, UNIFIL could not stop it or even delay it for very long. In reality what UNIFIL has been concerned with is *internal* security, and in this it has been quite effective. It has prevented the passage of "armed elements" through the area of operation, initially with less than 100 percent effectiveness (due in part to extensive hidden arms caches in the area that PLO elements could retrieve after entering it) but eventually with a high rate of success.

It has been a more difficult, if less hazardous, task to enhance the security of the inhabitants of the area—to protect them from the encroachment and pressures of internal elements and to do so without the powers of arrest or punishment. UNIFIL has done this in the first instance through the benevolent influence of its sheer presence. Its patrols have given continuing physical evidence of this. Force members have established and maintained contact with village leaders. UNIFIL repeatedly sought to curb attacks on villages within the area of operation by the South Lebanon Army and to prevent the entrenchment in the area of armed PLO elements. The physical presence of UNIFIL battalion outposts has afforded a sense of security evidenced by the impressive revival of villages located in their immediate vicinity. Compared to other rural areas in Lebanon, the entire UNIFIL area of operation is notable for its economic health, its new construction, and the rehabilitation of extensive farmland, although new destruction occurred during a fierce Israeli bombardment of Islamic fundamentalist centers in 1993.

UNIFIL has undertaken responsibilities normally belonging to the host government or local authorities. In particular it has controlled movement *within* Lebanon. It has performed police functions, receiving reports of civil offenses and turning them over to the most appropriate local authority available. In the earlier years after its deployment, UNIFIL participated actively in the restoration of essential services and in the rebuilding of houses, schools, and roads. Yet UNIFIL has never administered the area. It has drawn and maintained a careful line in this regard and in the process shown that a peacekeeping force can have significant—and beneficial—influence on an internal situation without having a mandate to administer. After the definitive Israeli withdrawal in 2000, the president of the Security Council issued a presidential statement reemphasizing that "the United Nations cannot assume law and order functions which are properly the responsibility of the Government of Lebanon. In this regard the Council welcomes the first steps taken by the Government of Lebanon and calls on it to proceed with the deployment of the Lebanese armed forces as soon as possible, with the assistance of UNIFIL, into the territory recently vacated by Israel."[17]

The third purpose for which UNIFIL was deployed was to assist the government of Lebanon in the restoration of its authority in the area. There are two ways in which UNIFIL has gone about this mandate. One is through the stabilization process just described, in which in the period prior to the second Israeli invasion UNIFIL cooperated with gendarmes remaining in the area and thus assisted an arm of the Lebanese government to exercise authority in the maintenance of law and order. By limiting the presence of forces hostile to the reassertion of the Lebanese government's authority in the area—the de facto forces in particular—UNIFIL contributed to a more hospitable environment in the area for the restoration of Lebanese authority. Finally, again prior to 1982, UNIFIL made it possible for elements of the Lebanese Army that were able to reach the UNIFIL area of operation to be stationed with UNIFIL units. When Israel occupied the area after the 1982 invasion, all evidence of the central government's authority disappeared. Now that Israeli forces have withdrawn and the de facto forces have disbanded the Lebanese Army is again present in the area; but UNIFIL remains deployed in southern Lebanon, albeit in reduced numbers, because the Lebanese forces are not able, alone, to maintain security along the border with Israel.

The situation in southern Lebanon poses a problem for peacekeepers that may well be present in other intrastate conflicts. UNIFIL was clearly deployed in support of the legitimate Lebanese government. Insofar as its mandate pertained to the external aspects of the problem—the presence of foreign forces—its desirable course of action was clear: to get the foreign troops out by observation, persuasion, and agreement on the withdrawal process. But how, in a situation of civil war, can a UN force act on behalf of the government when there are local elements hostile to the return of central control? In southern Lebanon the South Lebanon Army exercised military control except in the UNIFIL area, and even there its influence was palpable. A "Civil Administration" was created that functioned, under strong Israeli influence, as a kind of civilian arm of the South Lebanon Army. The village authorities contended that even if the Lebanese Army should be deployed in southern Lebanon, the United Nations should stay. This remains their preference now that the Lebanese Army and the Lebanese gendarmes have returned. The question of principle that emerges from this situation is: When a peacekeeping force has been deployed at the request of a legitimate government, how far should the force go in assisting the government to overcome domestic opposition to its authority?

This is the question that arose in an even more intense form in the Congo. At that time the secretary-general took the position that the secession of Katanga was essentially an internal matter and that the UN force should not be used to support the central government in bringing the secession to an end by military means. But in the end it did. In Lebanon a specific purpose of the UN deployment was to assist the government in restoring its authority. It was able to do this only to a limited extent in the area of UNIFIL operation and not at all in the area controlled by Israel and its surrogate, the South Lebanon Army.

NAMIBIA

The mandate of the UN peacekeeping operation in Namibia (UNTAG— the United Nations Transitional Assistance Group) was the most far-reaching and the most internally oriented ever given to a peacekeeping undertaking prior to the operations in Cambodia. In terms of international law, full responsibility for Namibia reverted to the United Nations (as successor to the League of Nations) following termination by the General Assembly in 1966 of South Africa's mandate to administer the territory of South West Africa. Therefore the UNTAG mandate could not be construed as authorizing intervention by the United Nations in the domestic affairs of a sovereign state. However, an allegedly independent government was in place and under the terms of the settlement agreement, incorporated in Security Council resolution 435 (1978), South Africa was authorized to administer, through an administrator-general, the elections that would be the key to Namibia's independence. So in reality UNTAG had responsibilities directly affecting the security and administration of Namibia, but actual authority to administer the territory rested with a local government and, for the elections, with South Africa.

Although military personnel were the largest element in UNTAG, its central purpose was political; namely, to establish conditions for the holding of free, universal elections in Namibia and to ensure that they were carried out in acceptable fashion. All of its responsibilities related to this central objective. These included:

- monitoring the cease-fire between the South West Africa People's Organization (SWAPO) and South African forces;

- monitoring the reduction and eventual removal of South African forces from Namibia and the return to civilian status in Namibia of SWAPO guerrillas;
- monitoring the borders to prevent infiltration;
- arranging for the release of political prisoners and the return of Namibians living in exile;
- ensuring that the remaining South African–organized South West Africa Police (SWAPOL) carried out their duties in a manner consistent with free and fair elections; and
- bringing about political and legal changes as necessary conditions for such elections and for the introduction of democratic government in a newly independent country.

The civilian and police (CIVPOL) elements of UNTAG became intimately involved in political developments and in the maintenance of security in the territory. Forty-two political offices were established throughout Namibia to work with the local administrative authorities in ensuring that the essential political processes took place. They performed in many instances a *conciliation* function by bringing black and white elements of the population together for meetings where they could discuss the stake that they shared in the successful transition to independence of their country. CIVPOL's primary function was to monitor the South-West African Police so that it would carry out its duty of maintaining law and order in an efficient and nonpartisan way. CIVPOL had no powers of arrest and could, in principle, influence the standard of policing only indirectly. Yet in the course of events it often patrolled on its own and was frequently present at political meetings when the local police authorities were not. The UN police function proved to be especially important in Namibia, and CIVPOL's size had to be increased during the operation. The military element of UNTAG was scaled down in size from original estimates and never reached even its scaled-down total.

Perhaps the most enduring UN influence on the domestic development of Namibia resulted from the legal advice given by UNTAG on the repeal of discriminatory legislation, on the enactment of legislation governing the elections, and on the drafting of the country's constitution. Many changes in the legislation and the constitution were made at UNTAG's insistence. The United Nations was intimately involved in both the political process leading to the elections and in supervising the entire electoral process. The secretary-general himself, during a visit to Namibia in July 1989, convened a meeting of all the political parties taking part in the elections and suggested that they meet regularly with the Special Representative of the Secretary-General to resolve any problems that might arise. The special representative subsequently worked out with the parties a political code of conduct that defined ground rules with which they voluntarily complied in their election campaigning.

Thus the UN peacekeeping operation in Namibia, which technically had neither enforcement nor administrative authority, actually performed a wide spectrum of functions that normally are within the responsibility of the national or local government. UNTAG controlled the borders; influenced the internal political process (without favoring any one political party); contributed to the maintenance of law and order and supervised the local police force; facilitated the return and resettlement of exiles; kept the population informed of developments through an active information program; and did much to determine the constitutional regime under which Namibia would be governed. As the United Nations itself has stated, UNTAG was deeply involved in the whole political process (which means the domestic process) of Namibia's transition from illegally occupied colony to sovereign and independent state.[18]

NICARAGUA

As part of the Central American Peace Process, the United Nations undertook three distinct actions with regard to Nicaragua. Together they can be seen as a major peacekeeping operation, which involved the United Nations very directly in domestic developments in a Member State.[19]

The first action to be undertaken, in November 1989, was the establishment of the United Nations Observer Group in Central American (ONUCA) by the Security Council.[20] Its mandate was (1) to verify the cessation of aid to irregular forces and insurrectionist movements; and (2) to verify the non-use of the territory of one state for attacks on other states. Consisting of unarmed military observers who carried out regular patrols by motor vehicles, helicopters, and patrol boats, ONUCA would seem to be in the classical peacekeeping tradition of border observation. But, significantly, ONUCA was not intended to prevent infiltration by national forces but rather by "irregular forces and insurrectionist movements"; that is, persons who, for the most part, were nationals of the country into which they would be infiltrating. Moreover, verification that the territory of one state is not being utilized for attacks on other states clearly involves intervention within the borders of sovereign states. The only previous comparable undertaking in UN peacekeeping history is the prevention of the transit of armed elements through the UN area of operations in southern Lebanon. Subsequently, the United Nations faced the problem of infiltration into Bosnia from Serbia of Bosnian-born Serb fighters, a problem that the peacekeeping operation there could not resolve.

The second UN action in the case of Nicaragua was the establishment of the International Support and Verification Commission (CIAV), the purpose of which was to make possible the voluntary demobilization, repatriation, or relocation in Nicaragua or third countries of the members of the Nicaraguan resistance and their families. The functions of CIAV, as stated in a joint plan agreed upon by the presidents of the five Central American countries, included good offices, disarmament and the custody of weapons, humanitarian assistance, and development aid. CIAV was established by joint decision of the secretaries-general of the UN and the Organization of American States (OAS), but in reporting to the Security Council, UN Secretary-General Pérez de Cuéllar noted that demobilization concerned the council "since it is an operation of a clearly military nature. . . . This is not a task that can be taken on by civilian personnel of the United Nations. . . . This task should be entrusted to military units equipped with defensive weapons. The launching of such an operation is clearly within the competence of the Security Council."[21] Subsequently the Security Council did authorize the use of such a military force, which was provided by Venezuela.

The monitoring of the national elections, held on February 25, 1991, was the third action with regard to Nicaragua undertaken by the United Nations. The United Nations Observer Mission for the Verification of the Elections in Nicaragua (ONUVEN) was established by the secretary-general in response to a request from the Nicaraguan minister for foreign affairs. The secretary-general acted within the terms of the General Assembly's earlier resolution calling on him to afford the fullest possible support to the peace process in Central America.[22] The mandate of ONUVEN went well beyond observing the elections. It included:

- verification that political parties were equitably represented in the Supreme Electoral Council;
- verification that political parties enjoyed complete freedom of organization and mobilization;
- verification that all political parties had equitable access to state television and radio; and
- verification that electoral rolls were properly drawn up.

Thus ONUVEN undertook the job of ensuring that the conditions within which the election campaign and the elections took place were satisfactory for free and fair elections. This went far beyond observing and reporting on the elections.

Technically, ONUVEN was not considered a peacekeeping operation because no military personnel were involved. Authorization of the Security Council was not required. In reality, however, it was an integral part of the overall UN effort to assist in the resolution of the internal conflict in Nicaragua. This conflict had evident implications for international security and for the peace of the region. There could be little doubt that the United Nations was acting in accordance with the first principle of the Charter, "to bring about by peaceful means, and in conformity with the principles of justice and international law, adjustment or settlement of international disputes or *situations* which might lead to a breach of the peace."[23] Yet the direct involvement of the United Nations in sensitive activities falling normally entirely within the domestic jurisdiction of a Member State constituted an added dimension to what the UN can do *in* Member States in pursuit of this principle.

HAITI

As was the case in Nicaragua, the government of Haiti in 1991 formally requested the United Nations to provide electoral assistance. The provisional government identified the holding of free, fair, and credible elections as a matter of top priority in ending the violence and instability that had plagued the country. The first response from the UN, undertaken at the initiative of the secretary-general, was the dispatch of a technical mission, financed by the United Nations Development Program, to help establish a credible and honest electoral process through technical and practical advice, practical training measures, and the exchange of experience with other developing countries. In addition, the secretary-general appointed a personal representative for Haiti and asked him to clarify further the Haitian request. In accordance with the clarifications that were subsequently received, which were communicated by the secretary-general both to the Security Council and to the General Assembly, the General Assembly by consensus[24] asked the secretary-general to meet the Haitian requests for: (1) electoral observers, (2) two or three security advisors to assist the Haitian Coordinating Committee for the Security of Electoral Activities, and (3) "specialized observers with solid experience in the field of public order." The result was the establishment of the United Nations Observer Group for the Verification of the Elections in Haiti (ONUVEH).

The role undertaken by the United Nations in Haiti constituted the first intervention in a Member State in which neither decolonization nor an immediate or evident threat to international security was involved. The security in question was internal. The need for the assistance requested by the Haitian government in this area was compelling. Nevertheless the introduction of "security" within a clearly internal context was widely seen as significant in terms of UN procedures. A case could be made—and was made by some experts within the Secretariat—that any security issue lay within the competence of the Security Council, especially if military officers were to be involved, as was unavoidable in the case of Haiti. However, there was strong resistance among Third World countries, especially in Latin America, to Security Council action to authorize election monitoring in Haiti because they saw in this the danger of affording the Permanent Members a precedent to intervene in the internal affairs of other small countries. Thus it was that the General Assembly took action on a matter involving security. For the record, ONUVEH, like ONUVEN, was not considered a peacekeeping operation even though military personnel were seconded to Haiti from UN peacekeeping operations elsewhere to serve as security observers. The General Assembly did not authorize funds for ONUVEH and the only available source was a contingency account for urgent needs related to international security. This account had been drawn on in the past largely, if not exclusively, for actions authorized by the Security Council. UN documents relating to the financing of ONUVEH fuzz the relationship between the funds used and international security.

Despite the evident sensitivity, ONUVEH did play an important part in the establishment of domestic conditions favorable for free elections. Responsibility for electoral security lay exclusively with the Haitian armed forces, but the UN advisors established close ties with the coordinating committee and participated in all of its preparatory work. They did similar service with local military authorities responsible for drawing up and implementing local security plans. The observers identified sensitive areas with a potential for conflict and by such action, and by their mere presence, stiffened the back of the responsible military authorities. ONUVEH assisted in ensuring coordination and understanding between the Haitian electoral and military authorities. Perhaps the most important of all "domestic" actions taken by ONUVEH was the so-called quick count of votes that it completed immediately after the balloting ended. This projection was so definitive on the election results that it discouraged any temptation on the part of candidates to challenge the election before the official results were announced a week later.

The UN electoral team left Haiti immediately after the electoral process was successfully completed. Unfortunately, the free election of a government after so many years of dictatorship was not sufficient to establish a sound basis for democracy. The freely elected government of President Jean-Bertrand Aristide was quickly overthrown. Having done too little to strengthen democratic institutions, the United Nations, along with Member States, subsequently faced the even more difficult problem of restoring a democratic government after a military regime was in power. Enforcement measures in the form of economic sanctions under Chapter VII of the Charter were imposed, and when they did not succeed, the use of military force under U.S. leadership had to be authorized in order to remove the military dictatorship and restore the legitimately elected president. Even this did not bring sustainable democratic governance to Haiti, but this was a failure of peace-building rather than of peacekeeping.

PAST EXPERIENCE AS A GUIDE FOR THE FUTURE

As is apparent from the foregoing review, UN peacekeeping operations in situations of intrastate conflict have a long history. The history has continued in Cambodia, Somalia, Bosnia, Mozambique, Sierra Leone, Kosovo, East Timor, the Democratic Republic of the Congo, and certainly in more cases yet to come. Some of these operations have been successful in stabilizing domestic situations by preventing a renewal of internal armed conflict (Cyprus, Cambodia); strengthening infrastructure (the Congo, Mozambique); improving local security (southern Lebanon, Kosovo); or facilitating an electoral process intended to lead to political stability, a result achieved in Nicaragua, El Salvador, Namibia, and East Timor but, unfortunately, not in Haiti or Somalia. It has been shown that simply by its presence, the United Nations can alter the conditions in which an electoral process takes place and contribute substantially to the success of elections. A Secretariat official who participated in the Haiti operation has observed that the presence of the UN introduces a transparency that has two beneficial consequences: it encourages the authorities charged with the organization and security of the electoral process to meet their responsibilities fully; and at the same time it discourages those who might be tempted to interfere with the electoral process or falsify the results. But the UN's experience has shown that free elections do not alone guarantee the successful democratization of a country that has undergone civil war, dictatorship, or the collapse of governmental institutions.

While the United Nations is by no means the only organization that has been asked by governments to observe elections, governments have shown that they attach special value to UN participation as being totally objective and trustworthy. Thus the government of Haiti invited the OAS and a number of nongovernmental organizations to observe its elections as well as the UN, but it requested only the UN to provide security advisers and security observers. This was the internally most sensitive function for a non-Haitian agency to undertake and was of critical importance to the success of the elections.

Through such stabilizing actions, UN peacekeeping operations in domestic conflict situations frequently perform a highly important postconflict peace-building role by reducing the causes of the social tensions that have given rise to conflict within a society. The strengthening of democratic processes, conciliation among population groups, the encouragement of respect for human rights (as specifically mandated in El Salvador and Cambodia), and the alleviation of humanitarian problems (as in Bosnia and Sierra Leone) are all part of this process. By carrying out such functions in a country seriously threatened by strife before conflict begins, the deployment of peacekeeping forces can also serve a deterrent purpose, enhancing the conflict prevention capacity of the United Nations. In intrastate conflicts the process of peacekeeping can, in itself, be part of a peace-building process. This was already true in the Congo, where the UN sought, not always successfully, to bring the various leaders together and in the end did contribute to conciliation and the maintenance of national unity. It was true in Namibia, where, as we have seen, the functions of the peacekeeping force were central to the establishment of a constitutional system and a freely elected government that became the basis of an internally peaceful country. Moreover, members of the peacekeeping operation in Namibia sought, with success, to conciliate elements within the society that had traditionally viewed each other with hostility. In Nicaragua the modalities were different but the effect quite similar. UN assistance in the strengthening of democratic procedures and institutions, in conjunction with the holding of free elections, should be seen as an essential part of this peace-building process within domestic societies.

This must be taken into account as the UN role in conflict deterrence and peace-building is pursued. Depending on the circumstances in a particular country, a UN peacekeeping operation should be equipped to promote conciliation between hostile groups, contribute to fair and constructive civil administration, and encourage respect for human rights. To meet such responsibilities, military and civilian peacekeeping personnel need more knowledge and sensitivity concerning the area where they are deployed and its inhabitants than has generally been the case until now. This again underlines the importance of obtaining extensive information on the political, social, and economic circumstances and of analysis and planning before an intrastate peacekeeping operation is undertaken.

If UN personnel are to be involved in elections, they need special training on the procedures involved. Some training is given to Secretariat personnel involved in such missions, but no way has yet been developed to give training to the military and police components aside from what may be provided by their own governments prior to deployment. The United Nations has amassed valuable experience by now and is in a position to give training courses and to teach others to do so, regional organizations in particular. Training for Secretariat components could be institutionalized at UN headquarters. Training could also be provided by UN staff members to military and civilian police components at training camps that several governments have offered to make available or, if no alternative is available, at the place of deployment.

For deployment in situations of internal tension, a peacekeeping force, in addition to having had specialized training, should include experts on the country or region who, as circumstances permit, can work for conciliation between hostile groups and advise the force commander concerning the conduct of the operation within the prevailing circumstances. The United Nations follows the practice of designating a "lead" agency to organize humanitarian assistance in conjunction with peacekeeping operations. Given the large numbers of refugees created by the dissolution of the former Yugoslavia, the United Nations High Commissioner for Refugees was designated to lead the humanitarian effort in that area, just as had been done almost twenty years earlier in Cyprus. This has proved largely effective, notwithstanding some problems in communication and coordination. This practice can be perfected and expanded. Liaison and coordination procedures at headquarters and in the field between the peacekeeping force and any functional agencies operating in the country or region should be institutionalized so that all available resources can be mobilized to meet the objectives of the operation. This was strongly recommended in the comprehensive and influential UN report on peacekeeping prepared in 2000 under the leadership of Lakhdar Brahimi.[25]

Complex, potentially dangerous intrastate peacekeeping operations such as the United Nations has undertaken in the former Yugoslavia, in Cambodia, and in Somalia demand disciplined, well-trained personnel equipped with modern communications capability. One advantage that derives from the end of the cold war is that the former inhibitions against utilization of troops from the five Permanent Members have fallen away. Russia, the United Kingdom, and France have all provided contingents for the peacekeeping operation in Bosnia and Herzegovina and Croatia, China provided an engineer battalion in Cambodia, and the United States led the peace enforcement operation in Somalia and contributed forces to the preventive peacekeeping operation in Macedonia. NATO and the Western European Union (WEU) worked together in applying naval measures to prevent the sanctions imposed by the Security Council against the former Yugoslavia from being broken. NATO eventually assumed the major responsibility for peace enforcement in Bosnia and Herzegovina. The availability of troops from these sources, while it can involve special problems, has substantially strengthened the capacity of the United Nations to meet new peacekeeping demands.

As intrastate peacekeeping expands, account has to be taken of the resistance of Member States to any threat to national sovereignty that a peacekeeping operation involved in essentially domestic matters might entail. In this context, it would be helpful if the principle could be established, perhaps through a General Assembly debate on a report submitted by the secretary-general, *that peacekeeping action undertaken at the request of, or with the consent of, the government of the country of deployment cannot, in itself, violate the country's sovereignty.*

In discussing peacekeeping, the concentration has been on intrastate conflict situations because that is the field in which there has been the greatest expansion of peacekeeping and it is also the most sensitive. It deserves to be reiterated here, however, that peacekeeping can also be used to deter conflict between states, as has been done successfully in Macedonia. There has been evidence in Cyprus and southern Lebanon, however, that a lightly armed peacekeeping force cannot prevent a fully armed and determined force from invading. Therefore any such preventive deployment should be accompanied by a commitment of the Security Council to take appropriate measures under Chapter VII of the Charter if the peacekeeping force is attacked.

NOTES

1. UN document 998 (ES-I), 4 November 1956.
2. UN document S/4382 (1960).

3. SC/RES/13 (1960).

4. The Congo became a member of the United Nations on 20 September 1960.

5. UN document S/4389 (1960).

6. Interview with Major General Indar Jit Rikhye, UN Oral History Collection, Yale University Library.

7. S/RES/161 (1961).

8. OR, SC, 940th meeting, paragraphs 2–7; SG/1012, 20 February 1961 (S/4727/add.2, Annex 4).

9. See Brian Urquhart, *Dag Hammarskjold,* New York: Harper and Row, 1984, p. 402.

10. S/RES/186 (1964).

11. UN document S/5950 (1964).

12. Ibid.

13. Ibid.

14. UN document S/21982 (1990).

15. S/RES/425 (1978).

16. See *The Blue Helmets* (New York: United Nations, 1996); also Report of the Secretary-General S/12611.

17. S/PRST/2000/21, 18 June 2002.

18. United Nations, *The Blue Helmets*, p. 385.

19. As part of the Central American Peace Process the UN is also involved in facilitating resolution of internal conflicts in El Salvador and (less directly) Guatemala.

20. S/RES/644 (1989).

21. Letter dated 28 August 1989 from the UN secretary-general to the president of the Security Council.

22. A/RES/43/24 (1988).

23. UN Charter Chapter I, Article 1. Italics added for emphasis.

24. A/RES/45/2 (1990).

25. UN document A/55/305-S/2000/809, 21 August 2000.

Chapter 4

REPELLING AGGRESSION AND ENFORCING PEACE

MEETING AGGRESSION WITH MILITARY FORCE

There are two types of military enforcement action in which the United Nations can engage in the interest of peace. The first is action taken against an aggressor who has broken the peace or threatened to do so. This was seen at the time it was founded as the only justification for resort by the United Nations to military force. The UN Charter gives the Security Council the authority "to maintain or restore international peace and security" and to enforce the will of the council on a state that has broken the peace. If peaceful means of dispute settlement, as described in Chapter VI of the Charter fail, the Security Council may decide on sanctions to give effect to its decisions, and if these also prove inadequate it may take military action. This use of force can best be identified as an Article 42 enforcement action because that article authorizes the council to take "such action by air, sea or land forces as may be necessary to maintain or restore international peace and security."[1] In such cases, the council does not act as a neutral agent to bring an end to conflict between two warring parties but, rather, as a party, itself, acts to defeat a country or countries whose guilt has been established by council decision and to protect the threatened party. This provides the means whereby countries can, in theory, be protected by the United Nations from aggression through utilization of armed force.

According to Article 43 of the Charter, all UN members undertake "to make available to the Security Council on its call and in accordance with a special agreement or agreements, armed forces, assistance and facilities, including rights of passage, necessary for the purpose of maintaining international peace and security." There are no specified restrictions on the type or extent of force to be used for these purposes. In the first years of the United Nations, the Military Staff Committee, at the direction of the Security Council, sought to reach agreement on how Article 43 should be implemented; it eventually produced a report, "General Principles Governing the Organization of Armed Forces Made Available to the Security Council by Member Nations."[2] However, primarily because of wide differences between the United States and the Soviet Union on the structure and mission of the forces to be made available to the Security Council, key issues remained unresolved. No agreements were ever reached and no troops for use by the council, as foreseen in the passages quoted from the Charter, have been available. Therefore, in the only two instances in which Article 42–type action has been taken, the Security Council has called for, or authorized, the use of forces under national command to *enforce* the council's resolutions.

KOREA

When North Korea attacked South Korea in 1950, the Security Council, in the temporary absence of the Soviet Union (which was boycotting the council on the question of Chinese representation), adopted a resolution that identified the North Korean act as aggression and called on Member States to assist South Korea in resisting it. The council recommended that "all Members providing military forces and other assistance pursuant to the . . . [relevant] Security Council resolutions make such forces and other assistance available to a unified command under the United States."[3] It requested further that the United States designate the commander of such forces and it authorized use of the UN flag by the unified command. Thus, in the case of Korea the Security Council requested one Member State to lead a combined effort on behalf of the United Nations to resist aggression by force. Notwithstanding his designation as commander of the unified forces in Korea, neither General Douglas MacArthur nor his successors ever sought or received instructions or guidance from the Security Council on the conduct of the war. The Military Staff Committee, which is mandated under the UN Charter to assist the Security Council in making plans "for the application of armed force" and to "advise and assist the Security Council on all questions relating to the Security Council's military requirements for the maintenance of peace and security . . ."[4] had no role in directing military operations in Korea. Neither did the council itself.

The General Assembly, however, established a three-nation cease-fire committee that sought a formula to end the war, and the secretary-general suggested the procedure of direct talks between the military commanders that was ultimately followed. Through this procedure an armistice—but not peace—was achieved. As in the case of the military campaign, the commander of the unified forces in Korea carried out the protracted armistice negotiations on the basis of instructions from Washington, not from the United Nations.

The advantages offered by the Korean procedure were:

- Expeditious action to resist aggression. Only the United States had troops in East Asia that could be rapidly deployed for quick military action in Korea.

- The unambiguous command structure needed for large-scale field operations.

- A practical way to meet the responsibilities of the United Nations under the Charter in the absence of the multilateral force foreseen in Article 43.

- Validation of the concept of collective response to aggression. States acted jointly in response to Security Council (and subsequent General Assembly) decisions to defend a country under attack even though the country was not a UN member.

The disadvantages of this procedure (which became more evident in the course of time) were:

- Lack of UN control or influence over the course of military action or over the precise purposes for which it was exercised (e.g., to repel and punish aggression or to reunify the peninsula under a freely elected government.)

- Identification of the military operation with the policy of the nation leading the effort rather than with the United Nations.

- The encouragement of division within the United Nations. Resistance grew to the dominant role of one Member State pursuing goals not universally shared. Eventually a majority of Member States disassociated themselves from the UN military role in Korea.

- The possibility for the aggressor to portray the collective action as the action of one country, the United States, rather than the response of the international community as a whole.

All of these disadvantages were intensified in the Korean case by the bitter disagreements that prevailed at the time between the United States and both the Soviet Union and the People's Republic of China. Under conditions of harmony among the Permanent Members of the Security Council, these various disadvantages can have considerably less force, as was the case in the Gulf War, but they are not likely to be eliminated.

In the years between the Korean War and the Iraqi invasion of Kuwait, the United Nations did not respond militarily to threats to the peace or acts of aggression. Even on those rare occasions when the United States and the Soviet Union were in agreement during the cold war, as in the Suez crisis in 1956, no UN army was fielded under Chapter VII of the UN Charter to *force* an invading army to withdraw. Peacekeeping was developed as a means of stabilizing a postconflict situation or, as described in the previous chapter, a preconflict situation in the Congo. It was characterized by Secretary-General Dag Hammarskjöld, who first deployed a true peacekeeping force, as a provisional measure under Article 40 of the Charter. According to this article the Security Council may call upon the parties concerned to comply with such provisional measures as it deems necessary or desirable, such provisional measures being "without prejudice to the rights, claims or position of the parties concerned." In peacekeeping the United Nations does not act as a party *against* another party as under Article 42 but, rather, as a force to stabilize the situation, without taking sides.

Only with the profound change in Soviet policy that led to an end of the cold war did the necessary extent of agreement develop among the Permanent Members of the Security Council to permit resorting to force in accordance with the principle of collective security.

KUWAIT

When Saddam Hussein initiated his action against Kuwait, the Permanent Members of the Security Council were in general agreement that it must be resisted. To this degree the circumstances were radically different from those that prevailed at the time of the North Korean invasion of South Korea. In another sense they remained the same: No armed forces were available for the Security Council to deploy under the terms of Article 42 of the Charter. No agreements had been completed with Member States on the provision of such troops.

Again, as in 1950, the Security Council relied on Member States to use force, acting independently of UN command, to repel the aggression of a state that had been branded as aggressor by the council. After imposing a comprehensive embargo in a fruitless effort to bring about Iraqi withdrawal and restoration of the legitimate government of Kuwait, the council first called upon "those member states co-operating with the government of Kuwait which are deploying maritime forces to the area to use such measures commensurate to the specific circumstances as may be necessary under the authority of the Security Council . . . to ensure strict implementation [of the embargo]."[5] Then, in resolution 678 of November 29, 1990, the Security Council authorized Member States "to use all necessary means" to uphold and implement the earlier council resolutions. All states were requested to provide appropriate support "for actions undertaken." This approach, taken with specific reference to Chapter VII of the Charter, constituted a modification of collective security as it had been implemented in Korea. As in the earlier enforcement action in Korea, the council again turned to Member States to act on its behalf through such measures as might be necessary. This time, however, no unified command was established, and the use of the UN flag was not authorized.

The Gulf enforcement action was possible because the Permanent Members of the Security Council cooperated on a matter of peace and security in the way originally foreseen when the United Nations was founded. Representatives of the United States and the former Soviet Union repeatedly suggested at the time that such action was an important element in a new world order—that is, a world in which nations would be safe because of the capacity of the United Nations to guarantee their security through collective measures. This fundamental goal of the United Nations was unquestionably brought closer through the sustained cooperation and a notably increased commonality of interests among the major powers. But serious questions remain as to (1) whether the approach taken in the Gulf War constitutes a desirable model to enforce the council's decisions under Article 42 of the Charter; (2) whether it could be successfully applied in other circumstances; and (3) whether other options exist.

With regard to the first question, the action taken by the council in response to the Iraqi aggression clearly constituted "effective collective measures for the prevention and removal of threats to the peace, and for the suppression of acts of aggression" as foreseen in Article 1 of the Charter. It authorized individual states to take "the necessary action" and it requested all states "to provide appropriate support for the actions undertaken." All states were called on to assist in defending a state from aggression as specifically foreseen in Chapter VII of the Charter. But the essential concept represented by Article 42 of the Charter is that troops and support will be available from Member States for *use by the Security Council*—a truly United Nations force. The procedure of calling on individual states to take the necessary enforcement action, without specified restrictions or limitations, represents a necessary improvisation. It gave the council, both in Korea and the Gulf, no means of controlling when, how, or in what degree the enforcement measures were applied. States were only requested to keep the council regularly informed.

Given the large extent of agreement on the need to repel Iraqi aggression that existed among the Permanent Members of the Security Council and the very strong diplomatic and military leadership exercised by the United States, no serious dissent arose with regard to the initial actions taken against Iraq by the Coalition forces. As the massively destructive campaign went forward under U.S. command, however, increasing unease became apparent among council members and the wider UN membership on the proportionality of the means being used to achieve the objectives. President George Herbert Walker Bush and the Coalition partners felt free to give their own interpretation to the Security Council resolutions. Had the United States decided to pursue the battle to Baghdad in order to eliminate Saddam Hussein, which might have been justified under a liberal interpretation of resolution 678, serious differences would have developed within the council and in the General Assembly. If support within the organization becomes fragmented, all the disadvantages that emerged from the Korean operation become operative. Moreover, if measures taken cease to have the endorsement of the majority of the Security Council, the question arises as to whether they can still be considered collective measures taken on the council's behalf. This is what happened when sanctions were maintained against Iraq over an extended period to force the regime to comply to the full satisfaction of all council members with the disarmament provisions of resolution 687.

In assessing the future viability of the approaches followed in Korea and the Persian Gulf, it must also be taken into account that they are not likely to be feasible unless the vital interests of one or more major military powers are at risk. When the NATO members decided that forceful, Article 42–type military action should be taken against Serbia to end genocidal attacks against the non-Serbian population of Kosovo, the Security Council was not asked to authorize the action because Russia was known to be opposed. The council agreed that the United Nations should assume responsibility for peace-building in Kosovo only after the military action against Serbia was completed. In 2003 when the United States, the United Kingdom, and Spain sought Security Council authorization for military action against Iraq to counter the threat to international security posed by Iraq's alleged possession of weapons of mass destruction, they were rebuffed.

OTHER OPTIONS

There clearly are alternative procedures that might be followed by the Security Council that offer the prospect of effective Article 42 enforcement action without according unrestricted responsibility to individual Member States or coalitions. One option would be a variant of the procedure followed in Korea. National forces could be brought together in ad hoc fashion under a unified UN command, with the commander designated by whichever happened to be the major troop-contributing country. The problems that arose in Korea could be alleviated if the unified commander were required to consult with the Security Council, or with some form of military authority established by the council, on the mission of the military operation and on the basic strategy to be followed in pursuing it. The United States has resisted such a practice, but its position may not be immutable as such a procedure would not give the council operational command over U.S. troops. It would have the distinct advantage of giving the Security Council a decisive voice in defining strategic objectives and in maintaining a close UN identification with all action taken. Moreover, it would lessen the possibility for the country or countries subject to the military action to create disunity in the Security Council. On the other hand, the exercise of strategic leadership by the council in a military campaign could prove cumbersome even when members are in agreement on ultimate goals.

Another theoretical option would be application of the procedure defined in Articles 42 and 43 of the Charter, as Secretary-General Boutros Boutros-Ghali suggested in *An Agenda for Peace.*[6] For this to be feasible, the special agreements foreseen in Article 43 of the Charter under which all members undertake "to make available to the Security Council on its call . . . armed forces, facilities and assistance" would have to be completed. Once such agreements were completed with a substantial number of Member States that maintain effective military establishments, the Security Council would be able to call into being a multilateral force (land, sea, and air) under a UN commander "to maintain or restore international peace and security." In such a military operation the commander appointed by the Security Council would have tactical authority but would operate under the guidance of the council or a body established by the council to serve this purpose. The Military Staff Committee, augmented by representatives of countries having a direct interest in the force, could, as foreseen when the Charter was drafted, "advise and assist the Security Council on all questions relating to military requirements." The committee, which functions on the basis of consensus, would not hold command authority. An enforcement operation using such troops would be clearly identified as a *UN* operation. Control would be firmly in the hands of the Security Council. The likelihood of sustained support among UN members for the action undertaken would be strong.

Taking account of the new opportunities that arose from the vast improvement in East-West relations, Boutros-Ghali recommended in *An Agenda for Peace* that the Security Council initiate negotiations on Article 43 agreements with willing states.[7] In doing so, he recognized that the Security Council might never be able to organize an enforcement operation against a country having a major military capacity such as Iraq had when it invaded Kuwait. But in circumstances involving aggression or a threat to peace by a state of only modest military power, such a UN force could be effective and might well be the only kind of force available to deal with the situation. The response among UN members to this suggestion was muted to say the least. Neither the General Assembly nor the Security Council, in their detailed and generally positive reviews of *An Agenda for Peace,* endorsed the proposal. In both organs the majority considered that it required "further study." The United States, in a presidential decision defining its policy on UN peace operations, expressed its opposition to entering into an Article 43 agreement with the United Nations.[8] None of the other Permanent Members of the Security Council has expressed interest in entering into such an agreement, and other states have generally been unwilling to negotiate before the Permanent Members agree to do so. It is thus unlikely that even in the improved atmosphere of the post–cold war era the multilateral earmarked fighting force foreseen in the Charter will be available to the council.[9] This option can for all practical purposes be ruled out.

A more realistic, but limited, option would be for the Security Council to call on regional organizations (rather than individual states) to undertake enforcement action as needed to meet threats to peace—something that would have been inconceivable during the cold war. This is foreseen in Chapter VIII, Article 53, of the UN Charter. The council successfully enlisted NATO air support to ensure the effective application of the sanctions imposed by the council against Yugoslavia and, subsequently, to enforce a no-fly zone and provide air protection for UN peacekeepers and for designated protected locations in Bosnia.[10] The threat of air attacks caused the Bosnian Serbs to stop their bombardment of Sarajevo and Gorazde, and NATO support proved effective elsewhere even though command and control arrangements were awkward. The U.S. presidential policy decision on UN peace operations states that the United States will support peacekeeping by regional organizations provided it is endorsed by the UN Security Council and is conducted in accordance with Security Council criteria.[11] Unfortunately, no regional organization comparable to NATO, on which the UN can call to undertake enforcement operations, exists in other geographic regions. Future possibilities in other areas are discussed in chapter 7 of this book on regional organizations.

PEACE ENFORCEMENT

As intrastate conflicts became prevalent beginning in the late 1980s, it became clear that in order to maintain peace, the United Nations needed the possibility of taking enforcement action of a different nature—action to enforce peace and security between parties within countries rather than to defeat an external aggressor. Repeatedly, in intrastate conflicts cease-fires were reached only to be ignored by the conflicting parties. This was true in Croatia, Bosnia and Herzegovina, Somalia, Angola, Rwanda, Sierra Leone, and in several of the new states in the former Soviet Union. It had been the long-standing rule for peacekeeping that deployment would not be authorized *until the cease-fire was demonstrably being honored*.[12] The result could be, and often was, continuation of the conflict. When the United Nations fails to take action in such cases, it appears impotent and incapable of fulfilling its first responsibility. Yet the reality was that the UN had no proper means of dealing with such situations.

To go into a country to stop the fighting between hostile elements who are intent on killing each other or on preventing the delivery of humanitarian assistance can be a dangerous undertaking. Third-party intervention can only be successful if the military force deployed is equipped with adequate arms not only to respond to attacks against it, but also to isolate the parties from each other, to take artillery out of action, to impound weapons, and to seal borders if arms are reaching one or both of the parties from external sources. This is far from the traditional peacekeeping mission and is not the kind of situation in which governments expect their troops to be placed if they are provided for peacekeeping. Countries such as Canada that have been most forthcoming in supporting peacekeeping operations have expressed the fear that public support will rapidly decline if their troops suffer serious casualties in a peacekeeping operation.

In situations where cease-fires are reached but not honored to the extreme danger of the civil population, something more than peacekeeping is needed. Yet these are not situations in which an aggressor can be identified and military force applied under the terms of Article 42 of the Charter. What is required is a force provided by Member States, to be deployed by authorization of the Security Council, not to fight against an aggressor but to force warring factions to comply with cease-fires to which they have agreed or to permit the delivery of humanitarian assistance without taking the side of one or the other.

To meet this problem, the concept of "peace enforcement" was developed.[13] As initially conceived, troops deployed for peace enforcement were to be authorized to take forceful action in order to bring combatants to comply with the terms of a cease-fire and to be adequately armed for this purpose. The concept was quickly expanded to cover the provision of humanitarian protection and even the restoration of democratic government. In *An Agenda for Peace,* Boutros-Ghali recommended that the Security Council "consider utilization of peace enforcement units in clearly defined circumstances and with their terms of reference specified in advance." He stated that such peace enforcement units would be available on call from Member States "and would consist of troops that have volunteered for such service. They would have to be more heavily armed than peacekeeping forces and would need to undergo extensive preparatory training within their national forces."[14]

Peacekeeping and peace enforcement missions as foreseen by the secretary-general are distinctly different. Both fall within the category of provisional measures in terms of Article 40 of the Charter; neither is intended to resolve the basic problems underlying a conflict; for both, deployment is decided by the Security Council, troops are provided on a voluntary basis by Member States, and operations are carried out under the management of the secretary-general. Peace enforcement troops, however, are mandated to take offensive action as necessary to restore peace. Obviously, different kinds of training are required in the two cases (although they could be mutually compatible), and governments, in earmarking peace enforcement units, would understand the more dangerous nature of their potential duty.

The reaction of Member States was initially cautiously positive to Boutros-Ghali's recommendation on peace enforcement units, but neither the Security Council nor the General Assembly officially endorsed the concept. It was nonetheless brought to reality by the force of events. The tragic conflicts in Somalia and Bosnia allowed no escape from the logic of the secretary-general's proposal. Developments there illustrated that conventional peacekeeping forces could not bring compliance with cease-fire agreements or afford adequate protection to ensure the safety of humanitarian operations under conditions of armed conflict or anarchy. Peace enforcement units, as defined in *An Agenda for Peace,* were needed. In the desperate situation of violence and conflict in Somalia, the Security Council approved actions on an ad hoc basis that amounted to realization of the peace enforcement concept. Unfortunately, the recognition of the need for peace enforcement came before the United Nations was adequately prepared for it.

YUGOSLAVIA

The inadequacy of traditional peacekeeping to halt a tragic conflict became evident when, with the breakup of the former Yugoslavia, fighting erupted between Croats and Serbs in newly independent Croatia. Given the high state of tension that existed throughout the former Yugoslavia, there was no doubt that the situation in Croatia (and briefly in Slovenia) constituted a threat to international security. UN action to restore peace was clearly called for. Action was delayed, however, and when it came it was inadequate.

No effort will be made here to recount in detail the complex course of events in which the United Nations was involved in the bitter ethnic strife that occurred in the former Yugoslavia. Instead, only the progression of developments that are directly relevant to the adequacy, or inadequacy, of the UN's efforts to bring an end to the fighting will be sketched.

It is necessary to begin in Croatia, where Croat and Serb forces after intense fighting reached repeated agreement on cease-fires and requested the United Nations to send a peacekeeping force. The request was rejected on the traditionally accepted ground that a peacekeeping force can only be deployed after a cease-fire is operative and the fighting has stopped. The fighting continued with increasing destruction and loss of life. Only after a cease-fire that held was reached through the mediation of a special UN envoy was a large peacekeeping force (UNPROFOR) sent to monitor its provisions. The force was, as is customary, equipped with light arms that it was authorized to use only in self-defense. While UNPROFOR was largely successful in preventing a recurrence of the fighting in Croatia, it was unable to overcome resistance of the parties to implementation of important provisions of the cease-fire such as the sequestering of all heavy weapons and the return of refugees.

UNPROFOR headquarters was established in Sarajevo. While it had no mandate with regard to Bosnia, the hope was that by its presence it would discourage the outbreak there of hostilities. Unfortunately, its presence did not have this effect. After civil war erupted in Bosnia and Herzegovina UNPROFOR headquarters was removed, leaving only 100 military and civilian staff in Sarajevo to promote local cease-fires (which were repeatedly achieved, only to be ignored) and humanitarian activities. Subsequently the UNPROFOR staff in Sarajevo was enlarged to secure the airport and to supervise the withdrawal of antiaircraft weapons and the collection of heavy weapons at agreed locations in the city.

UNPROFOR was initially mandated for action in Bosnia, as in Croatia, as a traditional peacekeeping force. It was authorized, as is normal in peacekeeping operations, to take such action as necessary against any attempt to prevent by force the carrying out of its mission. The mandate was subsequently strengthened to authorize the use of "all necessary means" to ensure delivery of humanitarian assistance.[15] However, the peacekeeping troops were too limited in number and inadequately armed to attempt to break through the indigenous forces that often blocked the transport routes and hampered relief operations. The UN troops remained *peacekeeping* forces. As such they could alleviate a desperate situation, but they could not provide the security needed for the uninterrupted delivery of relief assistance or to bring compliance with the repeated cease-fires that were reached in Sarajevo and elsewhere in the country.

While relying on peacekeeping troops on the ground, the Security Council, acting under Chapter VII of the Charter, imposed an embargo on arms shipments to all states of the former Yugoslavia[16] and comprehensive economic sanctions against Serbia and Montenegro. The situation in Bosnia nonetheless went from bad to worse.

Despite repeated Security Council resolutions demanding the cessation of Bosnian Serb attacks, the Serb bombardment of Sarajevo was intensified and isolated Bosnian Muslim centers were kept under siege. In the face of an increasingly desperate situation, the United Nations moved cautiously toward peace enforcement measures. The Security Council first called on states to take nationally, or through regional agencies, "all measures necessary" to facilitate the delivery of humanitarian assistance to Sarajevo and wherever needed in other parts of Bosnia.[17] This was an invitation to NATO to use air force against the attacking Bosnian Serbs. Countries having peacekeeping soldiers on the ground were fearful that they would be harmed as a result of such action, however, so none took place.

After repeated Security Council resolutions demanding the cessation of Bosnian Serb attacks were ignored, the council established a no-fly

zone over Bosnia to be enforced by NATO.[18] The council declared Sarajevo and the other besieged towns "safe areas, free from armed attacks
and from any other hostile acts which endanger the well-being and the
safety of their inhabitants."[19] The deployment of additional military observers was authorized to monitor the humanitarian situation in the safe
areas. A month later, the council decided that Member States, acting
nationally or through regional organizations, might take "all necessary
measures, through the use of air power, in and around the safe areas . . .
to support UNPROFOR in the performance of its mandate." At the same
time, the council expanded the UNPROFOR mandate to authorize it to
"take the necessary measures, including the use of force, in reply to
bombardments against the safe areas by any of the parties or to armed
incursion into them or in the event of any deliberate obstruction in or
around those areas to the freedom of movement of UNPROFOR or of
protected humanitarian convoys."[20]

The council took this action with direct reference to Chapter VII of
the Charter. The peacekeeping operation was thus altered in midstream
to a form of peace enforcement. But the troops remained too few and
inadequately armed to counter the Serb attacks on Sarajevo or even to
reach the other protected towns. Finally, when the situation in Sarajevo,
as shown on television around the world, became intolerable, the United
Nations gave an ultimatum to the Serbs to cease the bombardment of
the city and withdraw their heavy weapons to a distance of twelve miles
from the city or face air attacks by NATO. (NATO had already agreed
that it would take such action on request of the secretary-general.) This
enforcement threat had the desired effect as it did subsequently in
Gorazde, another besieged Bosnian "safe area," albeit not in the safe
area of Srebenica where the massacre of Muslim males despite the
presence of a UN peacekeeping detachment became a symbol of UN
ineffectiveness.

Peace enforcement action was taken in Bosnia without the presence of
sufficient UN forces deployed with a clear peace enforcement mandate.
The troops were provided by contributing countries for purely peacekeeping action. The contributors were therefore understandably reluctant to see
their contingents placed in the increased danger that enforcement involved. The Security Council troop deployments were unrealistically low
in terms of the conflict in the field. The result was a lack of clarity of
purpose and hesitancy in taking action that seriously jeopardized the
credibility of the United Nations and permitted the conflict to take an
unnecessary toll.

SOMALIA

Partly as a result of the experience in Croatia, the need for peace enforcement action was recognized at any earlier stage in the crisis in Somalia. Peace enforcement, as foreseen in *An Agenda for Peace,* was unambiguously authorized by the Security Council—for the first time in the UN's history—and knowingly undertaken by contributing states at the time of deployment. In March 1992 the United Nations, in association with the Organization of African Unity, the Arab League, and the Islamic Conference, succeeded in negotiating a cease-fire agreement between the principal warring factions in Mogadishu. The agreement provided for fifty unarmed UN military observers to monitor the cease-fire in Mogadishu and a UN security component for convoys of humanitarian assistance traveling to other points in the country. The security, or peacekeeping, force was to provide UN relief convoys with a sufficiently strong military escort to deter attack; but they were authorized to fire only in self-defense "as a last resort if deterrence should not prove effective."[21]

The factions did not comply with the cease-fire's provisions and the unarmed monitors had no means of forcing them to do so. A modest peacekeeping or "security" force, consisting of 500 Pakistani troops, was deployed to afford security for relief efforts in the capital. The force was largely immobilized by the violence and looting that dominated the city. In light of the deteriorating situation throughout the country, the Security Council approved the deployment of four additional UN security units, each with a strength of up to 750 troops, to be stationed in four operational zones of the country. In each there would be a consolidated UN effort to carry out relief and recovery programs; to monitor the cease-fire and contain potential hostilities; to oversee security, demobilization, and disarmament; and to encourage a peace process through conciliation, mediation, and good offices.

All in all the Security Council authorized the deployment of 4,219 peacekeeping troops to bring security in the conditions of anarchy and violence that engulfed the entire country. However, having only a peacekeeping mandate, they could not be deployed outside Mogadishu because various de facto Somali authorities refused to concur and conditions were such as to make the dispatch of lightly armed soldiers unacceptably dangerous. The major humanitarian effort that nongovernmental organizations and UN agencies were seeking to carry out came to a practical halt. Under these circumstances, action was taken that not only set an important precedent but provided a new definition of international security in the post–cold war world.

The U.S. government, spurred by the vivid media portrayal of the horrors of famine and violence in Somalia, informed Secretary-General Boutros-Ghali on November 25, 1992, that "if the Security Council were to decide to authorize Member States to use forceful means to ensure the delivery of relief supplies to the people of Somalia, the United States would be ready to take the lead in organizing and commanding such an operation."[22] The United States was prepared to provide as many as 32,000 troops for the enterprise. Just the day before, the secretary-general had addressed a letter to the Security Council president in which he described the gravity of the situation in Somalia. He ended by saying that "the conditions that have developed in Somalia . . . make it exceedingly difficult for the United Nations operation to achieve the objectives approved by the Security Council. I am giving urgent consideration to this state of affairs and do not exclude the possibility that it may become necessary to review the basic premises and principles of the United Nations effort in Somalia."[23] This is precisely what the U.S. action forced him and the Security Council to do. The question was posed: What can the United Nations legitimately undertake to stop an intrastate conflict or a major humanitarian catastrophe when traditional peacekeeping is inadequate? The secretary-general put this question to the Security Council in the form of five options:

1. To continue efforts to deploy a larger peacekeeping force, the United Nations Operation in Somalia (UNOSOM), that would operate according to the existing principles and practices of United Nations peacekeeping operations. (He did not feel this would be an adequate response to the humanitarian crisis in Somalia.)

2. To abandon the idea of using international military personnel to protect humanitarian activities, withdraw the existing peacekeeping force, UNOSOM, and leave the humanitarian agencies to negotiate the best arrangements they could with the various faction and clan leaders. (He excluded this "withdrawal" option with the conclusion that the current difficulties were due not to the presence of the peacekeepers but to the fact that not enough of them were there and they did not have the right mandate.)

3. To undertake a show of force with UNOSOM in Mogadishu in the expectation that this might create conditions there for the safe delivery of humanitarian relief and deter the various armed groups there and elsewhere in Somalia from withholding cooperation from UNOSOM.

4. To carry out a countrywide *enforcement* operation undertaken by a group of Member States authorized to do so by the Security Council.

5. To undertake a countrywide *enforcement* operation under United Nations command and control.

The secretary-general noted that the Secretariat did not have the capability to command and control an operation of the size and urgency required by the crisis. Member States contributing troops for the operation would therefore have to provide not only troops but also personnel for the command and control headquarters in the field and in New York. They would have to accept that the staff officers would take orders from the United Nations and not from their national authorities. Boutros-Ghali emphasized that there was no alternative but to resort to Chapter VII of the Charter, that is, *enforcement*. He preferred that if forceful action were taken, it be under UN command and control. If the fourth option were chosen, he suggested various means of linking the operation to the United Nations. The countries undertaking the action could be asked to furnish the Security Council with regular reports, for example, on the basis of which the council could, at specified intervals, review the authority it had given for the operation to take place. The council might also clearly establish the purpose of the operation and provide that as soon as the purpose was accomplished, the operation would be replaced by a UN peacekeeping operation. The secretary-general obviously had some of the unsatisfactory aspects of the conduct of the Gulf War in mind.[24]

The Security Council unanimously voted in favor of option four, welcoming the U.S. offer and authorizing the Member States "cooperating in implementation of the offer . . . *to use all necessary means* [i.e., force] to establish as soon as possible a secure environment for humanitarian relief operations in Somalia." In a notably vague paragraph, the council authorized the "Secretary-General and the member states concerned to make the necessary arrangements for the unified command and control of the forces involved which will reflect the [U.S.] offer referred to above."[25]

The United States informally proposed to carry out the action under the UN flag, but Boutros-Ghali opposed this on the ground that the UN would not actually be in control. The Somalia resolution contained the following preambular paragraph that is of major significance:

Determining that the magnitude of the human tragedy caused by the conflict in Somalia, further exacerbated by the obstacles being created for the quick distribution of humanitarian assistance, *constitutes a threat to international peace and security* [emphasis added].

This was the first time that an internal humanitarian crisis had been defined as a threat to international peace and security, justifying the use of enforcement measures under Chapter VII of the Charter. The use of all appropriate measures was authorized to *enforce* compliance with a cease-fire agreement and an end to violence as necessary to permit the safe delivery of humanitarian assistance. The mission of the U.S.-led Unified Task Force (UNITAF), was limited to establishing a secure environment for humanitarian relief operations in Somalia despite the strongly expressed views of Boutros-Ghali that it should also be responsible for disarming the various armed factions. The mission, having the advantage of the most modern arms and well-trained soldiers, was successfully accomplished with few casualties. Free movement for relief shipments was restored except for the northern, self-declared independent portion of Somalia, which had not been included in the UNITAF operation. Starvation was eliminated. In a complementary effort to establish a basis for peace, the secretary-general convened a preparatory meeting in Addis Ababa, Ethiopia, for a national reconciliation conference in which a total of fourteen Somali political movements took part. Agreement was reached on implementing the cease-fire and on modalities of disarmament. Subsequently, on March 15, 1993, the national reconciliation conference opened, also in Addis Ababa, and on March 27 the Addis Ababa Agreements were signed; they constituted the basis for the resolution of the political problems of Somalia. It appeared that the worst of the Somalia crisis might be over, although the extensive arms still in the hands of the various factions were an evident cause for concern.

In his proposals to the Security Council for the UN force to replace UNITAF, Boutros-Ghali recommended that the tasks of the replacement UN force, UNOSOM II, should include the following:

- Monitor compliance with the cessation of hostilities and all other agreements to which the parties have agreed.

- Take appropriate action against any faction that violates or threatens to violate the cessation of hostilities.

- Maintain control of the heavy weapons of the organized factions pending their destruction or transfer to a newly constituted national army.

- Seize the small arms of all unauthorized armed elements and assist in the registration and security of such arms.

- Maintain the security of all ports, airports and lines of communications required for the delivery of humanitarian assistance.

- Protect the personnel, installations and equipment of the UN and non-governmental humanitarian organizations *and take such forceful action as may be required to neutralize armed elements that attack, or threaten to attack, such facilities and personnel, pending the establishment of a new Somali police force which can assume this responsibility* [emphasis added].

- Continue the program for mine clearing.
- Assist in the repatriation of refugees and displaced persons within Somalia.[26]

This was a far broader and more difficult mandate than UNITAF had been given. In his report to the council Boutros-Ghali stated that the threat to international security that the Security Council had earlier found to exist still persisted. Consequently, in order to carry out these objectives UNOSOM II would have to be "endowed with enforcement powers under Chapter VII of the Charter."[27] The highest priority of UNOSOM II, however, was defined as support for the efforts of the Somali people "in promoting the process of national reconciliation and the establishment of democratic institutions."[28] The mission combined the military task of peace enforcement with the political task of peace-building. UNOSOM II was intended to establish, in conjunction with the Addis Ababa Agreements, a basis for the restoration of stable government in Somalia.

Thus the United Nations undertook for the first time a major *peace enforcement* operation under the control of the secretary-general, a concept that the Security Council had not (and still has not) approved in principle and one that the secretary-general said, at the time of the initial U.S.-led Somali operation, the United Nations was not equipped to carry out. This proved to be accurate, with extremely unfortunate consequences.

A number of conclusions can be drawn from this first UN-led peace enforcement undertaking that are of continuing relevance as the UN is involved more and more in the resolution of internal armed conflicts.

Impartiality

An essential requirement in peace enforcement, just as in peacekeeping, is strict impartiality. As a provisional measure, peace enforcement must be without prejudice to the rights, claims, or positions of the parties concerned. In Mogadishu, where the competing political leaders were resident with their separate militias, political impartiality was not—perhaps could not be—maintained.

General Mohamed Farah Aideed, the leader of a political faction known as the United Somali Congress, had long had a prominent role in Somali politics. He had taken the lead in unseating the Somali dictator Said Barre. He was well known to Secretary-General Boutros-Ghali as a disruptive element in Egyptian-led attempts to resolve the political crisis that followed the fall of Barre. Aideed had signed the cease-fire agreement along with his arch rival, but he did not cooperate with the UN observer and peacekeeping missions provided for in the agreement. In a report to the Security Council on November 27, 1992, the secretary-general identified General Aideed by name as responsible for a number of disturbing actions aimed at UNOSOM.[29] There was good reason, then, for the leaders of UNOSOM II to view Aideed with special concern. There was also a reasonable basis for Aideed to believe that the United Nations was hostile toward him. He is said to have known that the UN was secretly planning to capture his Mogadishu radio station. The U.S. Liaison Mission in Mogadishu, which was closely involved in the UN operation, appears inadvertently to have signaled to Aideed an intention to marginalize him and his clan.[30]

On June 4, 1993, UNOSOM officers informed Mohammed Hassan Awale Qaibdid, a close associate of General Aideed, that a designated weapons storage site in the same building as Aideed's radio station would be inspected the following day. Qaibdid responded that the inspection must not take place; if it did, it would lead to "war."[31] UNOSOM nonetheless proceeded with its plan. On the next morning UN soldiers trying to control a demonstration in front of Radio Mogadishu shot and killed a Somali. Shortly thereafter Pakistani forces were sent on the inspection mission in southern Mogadishu in unarmored vehicles despite the warning from Aideed's associate. Coming under coordinated attack, 24 troops were killed and more than 100 wounded, many seriously.

General Aideed claimed that the attacks on the UN troops were a spontaneous response to the killing of the Somali earlier in the day. The leaders of UNOSOM II concluded that the attack had been planned and executed by Aideed and his forces as an immediate response to the UN effort to inspect the weapons storage site but with the broader intent of crippling the UNOSOM II mission. An independent expert, Professor Tom Farer of American University, who was engaged by the UN special representative in Somalia, Admiral Jonathon Howe, to carry out an investigation, agreed. He found the UNOSOM conclusion valid and indisputable.[32]

The United Nations responded to the attack on the Pakistanis as a criminal act for which General Aideed was responsible. The UN decided to seek his arrest,[33] and it offered a monetary reward for assistance in finding the general. Once Aideed was categorized as an enemy, the UN action ceased to have the character of a provisional measure. A futile search for Aideed led to serious confrontations between the American peacekeepers and Somalis in which many Somalis were killed. The culmination was on October 3, when U.S. Rangers, on yet another mission to capture Aideed, were caught in a firefight with Somali militia. Seventeen Americans were killed and many more wounded. The number of Somalis killed is still not known.

The death of the Americans caused a strong outcry in the U.S. Congress and wide criticism in the media. Responding to these developments, President Bill Clinton gave orders to the U.S. forces in Somalia—without consulting the United Nations—to stop hunting Aideed. Subsequently, he announced that all U.S. forces would be withdrawn by the end of March 1994. The Security Council decided, in turn, that emphasis should again be placed on a political solution to the Somalia problem, implying that military enforcement measures would not be pursued. The effort to achieve disarmament by force was abandoned.[34] General Aideed emerged from hiding and was flown in an American plane to participate on equal terms in a further conference on national unity in Addis Ababa. There was no longer a designated enemy. But the unhappy developments that led to this return to impartiality had raised serious questions as to the viability of the concept of peace enforcement.

Familiarity with Culture and Politics

Peace enforcement and the successful building of peace in disintegrated societies require careful planning based on a full understanding of the culture and politics of the country or countries involved. This was not entirely absent in the Somalia operation, as evidenced by the considerable success achieved in restoring social stability in areas outside of Mogadishu.[35] At the political center, however, in Mogadishu, the inadequacy of the UN's preparation brought near disaster. The power and influence of the clan leaders was not adequately assessed nor was their individual importance in bringing about national reconciliation. The likely reaction of a man like General Aideed to actions that threatened the position of his clan was not sufficiently appreciated, nor was the reaction of the Somali population when a Somali leader was attacked by an outside force, which the United Nations remained.

Command and Control

There were clearly grave command and control failures in the UNOSOM II operation. There appears at times to have been no effective unified command at all. Various national contingents responded to orders from their national chains of command. The Italian contingent refused to follow the directives of the force commander. The authority of the secretary-general in the overall direction of the operation lacked credibility. Eventually, the Americans appeared to dominate the operation, acting largely independently of UN control (although a frequent criticism in the United States was that the U.S. forces were being endangered by serving under non-U.S. command).

Training

Peace enforcement requires special training. An obvious weakness of the Somalia military operation was the failure of the various national contingents to work effectively together. This was partly a command problem. But it also derived from the absence of common training on how to deal with volatile domestic situations. Neither the military nor the civilian leadership was adequately prepared for the problems inherent in enforcing peace in the absence of cooperation from one or more of the parties concerned. A 1994 study shows that in regular peacekeeping operations, the number of casualties in units that have had special training for peacekeeping service is far lower than in those that have not.[36] No similar study has been made of a peace enforcement action, but it is likely that positive effects of training would be shown to be even greater.

RWANDA

The failure of the United Nations to arrest the genocide in Rwanda, following closely on the failed peace operation in Somalia, reinforced the widely held impression that the UN was incapable of handling deadly internal conflicts. UN military involvement in Rwanda began in June 1993 when the Security Council authorized the deployment of the United Nations Observer Mission Uganda/Rwanda (UNOMUR) on the Ugandan side of the Uganda/Rwanda border to verify that no arms or other material of potential military use crossed the border into Rwanda.[37] At this time a civil war was already taking place between the government of Rwanda and the Tutsi-dominated Rwandese Patriotic Front (RPF), whose main forces were located in Uganda. UNOMUR was followed by the establishment of the United Nations Assistance Mission for Rwanda (UNAMIR),[38] which was deployed in Kigali in December 1993 for an initial period of six months with the proviso that its continuation would have to be reviewed by the Security Council after the initial ninety days. The principal functions of UNAMIR were to assist in ensuring the security of the capital; to monitor the cease-fire agreement, including the establishment of an expanded demilitarized zone; and demobilization procedures. It would investigate alleged noncompliance with provisions of the peace agreement. Furthermore, it would provide security for the repatriation of Rwandese refugees and displaced persons and assist in the coordination of humanitarian assistance activities. At the time of deployment, UNAMIR was to include 1,428 military persons plus 60 civilian police. After the formation of a transitional government, as foreseen in the Arusha peace agreement of August, 1993, between the Hutu-dominated Rwanda government and the Tutsi Rwandese Patriotic Front, the military contingent would rise to 2,548. Subsequently, it would be gradually reduced to 930 military personnel. In retrospect it can be seen that the size of the force was far too small to meet the assigned mandate within the increasingly tense conditions in Rwanda, about which the Special Representative of the Secretary-General in Rwanda and the force commander kept headquarters well informed. On April 6, 1994, a plane carrying the presidents of Rwanda and Burundi crashed at the Kigali airport, killing all on board. UNAMIR numbered 2,165 military at this point to face the genocidal conflict that then engulfed the country. With the departure of the Belgian contingent after Belgian soldiers were brutally murdered, the number of military personnel declined to 1,515 along with 190 military observers. UNAMIR was essentially impotent in the face of the continuing violence that engulfed the whole country. In these circumstances, the secretary-general put three alternatives to the Security Council. The first was immediate, massive reinforcement of UNAMIR and revision of its mandate to include enforcement powers under Chapter VII of the Charter with the purpose of averting further combat and massacres. The second alternative was to reduce UNAMIR to a small group that would remain in Kigali under the force commander to act as an intermediary between the two parties. The final alternative was the complete withdrawal of UNAMIR, an alternative that the secretary-general did not favor. The Security Council, in the midst of the ongoing genocide in Rwanda, voted to accept the second alternative. UNAMIR would be reduced to 970 military personnel. Its mandate was redefined to act as an intermediary between the parties; to assist in the resumption of humanitarian relief operations; and to monitor developments in Rwanda, including the safety and security of civilians who sought refuge with UNAMIR.

In May 1994, the Security Council authorized the expansion of UNAMIR to 5,500 troops and revised its mandate to enable it to contribute to the security and protection of refugees and civilians at risk. However, the secretary-general could not hope to deploy even the first phase of the expanded UNAMIR before July 1994 and could give no estimate of the date of further deployment because the necessary additional resources had not been made available. Under these circumstances, the council accepted France's offer to undertake a French-commanded, multinational operation under Chapter VII of the Charter to assure the security and protection of displaced persons and civilians at risk. The French-led action, which was called Operation Turquoise, led to the establishment of a humanitarian protected zone in southwestern Rwanda, covering about one-fifth of Rwandese territory. Many thousands of displaced persons found refuge there during the two months that the operation lasted, reportedly including a large number of Hutus who had been involved in the genocide. UNAMIR reached its full authorized strength of 5,500 troops only in October 1994, by which time the RPF had consolidated its position throughout Rwanda and established a new government. While more than a million additional people had fled the country and internal social conditions were deplorable, the civil war, with its massive slaughter, had ended.

This extremely sketchy account of UN involvement during the horrendous events that decimated Rwanda in 1994 can serve mainly as a framework for the question "what went wrong?" In March 1999 Secretary-General Kofi Annan, who had been Under-Secretary-General for Peacekeeping Operations at the time of the Rwanda debacle, appointed an "Independent Inquiry into the Actions of the United Nations during the 1994 Genocide in Rwanda" under the chairmanship of Ingvar Carlsson, the former prime minister of Sweden. Members of the inquiry carried out a comprehensive six-month investigation. The sixty-seven-page report that they produced provides a candid and comprehensive answer to the above question.[39]

The inquiry members concluded that a lack of resources and a lack of the necessary commitment to prevent genocide constituted the "overriding failure" underlying what happened in Rwanda. According to the report, UNAMIR

> was not planned, dimensioned, deployed or instructed in a way that provided for a proactive and assertive role in dealing with a peace process in serious trouble. The mission was smaller than the original recommendations from the field suggested. It was slow in being set up, and was beset by debilitating administrative difficulties. It lacked well-trained troops and functioning matériel. The mission's mandate was based on an analysis of the peace process, which proved erroneous, and which was never corrected despite the significant warning signs that the mandate had become inade-

quate. By the time the genocide started, the mission was not functioning as a cohesive whole: in the real hours and days of deepest crisis, consistent testimony points at a lack of political leadership, lack of military capacity, severe problems of command and control and lack of coordination and discipline.

The chairman, Carlsson, stated at a press conference introducing the report that it would "always be difficult to explain" why the United Nations decided to reduce its peacekeeping troop presence in Rwanda once the genocide had started and increase it again once it was over.[40]

The inquiry concluded that responsibility for the inadequacy of the UN's performance in Rwanda was shared by Member States, the Security Council, the Secretariat, and the field mission. It put forward many recommendations, including the following, addressed to each:

- Renewed efforts should be made to improve the UN's capacity in the field of peacekeeping, including the availability of resources.
- The Security Council and troop-contributing countries must be prepared to act to prevent acts of genocide or gross violations of human rights wherever they take place.
- In each peacekeeping operation it should be clear which rules of engagement apply.
- The early warning capacity of the United Nations needs to be improved.
- An effective flow of information needs to be ensured within the UN system.
- National evacuation operations should be coordinated with missions on the ground.

Similar recommendations were to be repeated in the subsequent Brahimi report on peacekeeping, to which reference has already been made.

WHITHER PEACE ENFORCEMENT?

There has been widespread criticism of the ineffective utilization of peacekeeping forces by the United Nations in Bosnia, Somalia, and Rwanda. From the foregoing accounts, it is evident that serious mistakes were made in all three cases. It is instructive to note, however, that criticism of the operations is, in very general terms, based on opposite grounds. In the cases of Bosnia and Rwanda, the charge (with which the author concurs) is that the enforcement measures taken were too little and too late. In the case of Somalia, the charge is that enforcement efforts were precipitate and impractical (an assessment that this observer considers shortsighted).

It appears beyond question that the traditional peacekeeping mandate was inadequate to bring an end to the fighting in the former Yugoslavia. The credible threat of the application of strong military force was necessary in order to stop the Serb attacks. The transition from an operation conceived as peacekeeping to an enforcement action ("mission creep") complicated the operation, suggesting the need for careful assessment and planning before an operation is initiated in an intrastate conflict.

In Somalia the initial peace enforcement action, UNITAF, was highly successful, achieving quick results that a classic peacekeeping operation almost certainly could not have done. Peacekeeping had been demonstrably incapable of maintaining the cease-fire in Mogadishu. For this purpose, enforcement measures were also needed.

From these two experiences the conclusion emerged—and was subsequently reinforced by the disastrous UN experience in Rwanda—that peace enforcement is a much-needed addition to the tools available to the United Nations in seeking to end internal conflict. It also emerged that the United Nations and Member States had much to learn, and many adjustments to make, in applying the concept in the future. Taking account of these experiences, Secretary-General Boutros-Ghali issued a *Supplement* to *An Agenda for Peace,* in which he amplified and, to a certain extent, stepped back from his earlier recommendations.[41] "Nothing," he concluded, "is more dangerous for a peace-keeping operation than to ask it to use force when its existing composition, armament, logistic support and deployment deny it the capacity to do so." On the critical problem of command and control, which had failed badly in Somalia, he states that

it is useful to distinguish three levels of authority:

   a. Overall political direction, which belongs to the Security Council;
   b. Executive direction and command, for which the Secretary-General is responsible;
   c. Command in the field, which is entrusted by the Secretary-General to the chief of mission (special representative or force commander/chief military observer).

Having defined these three levels, Boutros-Ghali goes on to say that "neither the Security Council nor the Secretary-General at present has the capacity to deploy, direct, command and control operations for this purpose [enforcement], except perhaps on a very limited scale. . . . It would be folly to attempt to do so at the present time when the Organization is resource-starved and hard pressed to handle the less demanding peacemaking and peace-keeping responsibilities entrusted to it."[42] Boutros-Ghali was recommending what most of his peacekeeping staff in the Secretariat had concluded: that military enforcement action, whether peace enforcement or Article 42 action, should be implemented by Member States (coalitions of the willing) under national command with the authorization of the Security Council. This had proved successful in the UNITAF action in Somalia and in Haiti and would later be successful when Australia took the lead in organizing a peace enforcement action in East Timor. Unfortunately there are not always Member States willing to take the lead in organizing and implementing an enforcement action, as would be the case in Sierra Leone, where the UN-led enforcement action ran into grave difficulties until an independently organized British force arrived to stabilize the situation.

It must be stated that progress has been made in the Secretariat for managing peace operations in their various dimensions. A state-of-the-art operations center has been established at UN headquarters through which constant communication with field operations is now possible. Additional posts have been added to the Department of Peacekeeping Operations. The importance of pursuing a political track simultaneously with peace enforcement measures is now better understood, as is the need for fuller background information on the historical, social, and political circumstances in deciding whether peacekeeping or peace enforcement is the right course to follow. A fair number of Member States have signed agreements with the United Nations to hold specified numbers of troops in readiness for deployment at the request of the secretary-general. Increased amounts of equipment needed for quick action are being stored in various regional depots. Even with these agreements in place, much still depends on the willingness of governments to make the designated troops available in specific cases. No agreement covers the provision of troops for enforcement purposes. And the most powerful country, the United States, remains unwilling to sign any agreement at all. So while much has been learned, and the secretary-general is better equipped than before the present millennium to deploy and manage peacekeeping and peace enforcement actions, the availability of military and police forces still depends on national decisions and is subject to national interests.

NOTES

1. UN Charter, Article 42.
2. SCOR 2nd Year, Special Supplement #1, S/336.

3. S/RES/84 (1950).

4. UN Charter, Article 47.

5. S/RES/665 (1990).

6. Boutros Boutros-Ghali, *An Agenda for Peace* (New York: United Nations, 1995), pp. 55–56.

7. Ibid., p. 56.

8. Presidential Decision Directive 25, Federal Register Volume 59, 3 May 1994.

9. In 1992, the Foreign Relations Committee of the U.S. Senate expressed strong support for the negotiation of an Article 43 agreement between the United States and the United Nations. This was not endorsed, however, by the full Senate.

10. See S/RES/824 (1993), S/RES/836 (1993), S/RES/844 (1993), and S/RES/908 (1994).

11. The NATO treaty refers to Article 51 (the right of self-defense) but makes no mention of Article 53. When the U.S. Senate was considering ratification of the NATO treaty, Secretary of State Dean Acheson testified that NATO would not be subject to orders of the Security Council. This appears to be the accepted principle, and the availability of NATO forces will always be dependent on the agreement of the NATO Council. In the Croatian and Bosnian cases, the relevant Security Council resolutions refer to the participation of regional organizations in enforcement as voluntary.

12. This principle is specifically endorsed in Presidential Decision Directive 25.

13. Other terminology is frequently used to designate "peace enforcement." Secretary-General Kofi Annan refers to "coercive inducement." Others refer to "second generation peacekeeping." Whatever words are used, the concept is the same.

14. Boutros Boutros-Ghali, *An Agenda for Peace,* p. 57. The earmarking and training of troops and the stockpiling of equipment for such a purpose is not an entirely new idea. During the Korean War the General Assembly recommended that each Member Sate maintain within its armed forces earmarked units so trained that they could promptly be made available for service as a United Nations unit or units. This was before the peacekeeping concept was developed. Presumably, therefore, these troops were foreseen for enforcement purposes, although it was not specifically so stated. In any event, Member States did not comply with the recommendation. Subsequent recommendations by secretaries-general and various external organizations were for the earmarking and training only of *peacekeeping* forces.

15. S/RES/871 (1993).

16. S/RES/713 (1992).

17. S/RES/770 (1992).

18. S/RES/781 (1992).

19. S/RES/824 (1993).

20. S/RES/836 (1993).

21. See S/RES/751 (1992) establishing the United Nations Operation in Somalia (UNOSOM).

22. UN document S/24868, 30 November 1992.

23. UN document S/24859 (1992).

24. UN document S/24868 (1992).

25. S/RES/794 (1992).

26. UN document S/25354 (1993).

27. Ibid.

28. Cited in S/RES/886 (1993).

29. UN document S/24859, 27 November 1992.

30. See "From Warlord to Peacelord" in the *Washington Post,* 12 September 1993, by Tom Farer.

31. "UNOSOM II Assessing Success and Failures" (New York: Friedrich Ebert Foundation, 1993).

32. UN document S/26351, 24 August 1993.

33. S/RES/837 (1993).

34. S/RES/897 (1994).

35. See Report of the Secretary-General to the Security Council S/1994/12, 6 January 1994.

36. Barry M. Blechman and J. Matthew Vaccaro, "Training for Peacekeeping: The United Nations' Role" (Washington, D.C.: Henry L. Stimson Center, 1994).

37. S/RES/846 (1993).

38. S/RES/872 (1993).

39. *Report of the Independent Inquiry into the Actions of the United Nations during the Genocide in Rwanda,* 15 December 1999, pp. 23–24 and 42–43. Available from http://www.un.org/News/ossg/rwanda_report.htm

40. Press briefing 16 December 1999. Press conference on Report of Rwanda Inquiry Team. United Nations Department of Public Information.

41. The *Supplement* is in A/50/60-S/1995/1, 3 January 1995, and is included in the edition of *An Agenda for Peace* published by the UN in 1995.

42. Boutros-Ghali, *Supplement* to *An Agenda for Peace,* pp. 15–16.

Chapter 5

BUILDING PEACE

Preventive diplomacy is generally seen—as it has been in chapter 2 of this book—as action to be taken in response to a critical situation that threatens to lead to conflict. The prevention of conflict, however, has a larger dimension. Over the long term, the surest way to prevent conflict is to eliminate its root causes. Conditions of life must be achieved that will permit peoples to live in harmony with each other under democratic governance that in itself will serve as a deterrent to war.[1] The term *peace-building* has come into use to describe what needs to be done to bring about these conditions, or, at least, to make progress toward this goal. Peace-building can be seen as the macro approach to the prevention of war. It can too easily be dismissed as overly idealistic and vague, as beyond the human capacity and certainly beyond that of existing multilateral organizations, but it has been increasingly emphasized as the United Nations has encountered serious difficulties in resolving internal conflicts once they have become violent.

The danger is apparent of conflict, often intrastate in nature, that results from social and economic causes, and of humanitarian disasters that in their consequences can be equated with war. With the end of the cold war, more resources and greater attention should, in principle, have been available to alleviate these problems than has been the case since the United Nations was founded. There is evidence that the disappearance of the rivalry between the United States and the Soviet Union has resulted in *less* rather than more attention being paid to the needs of the poorer countries as the United States and the Soviet Union are no longer competing for strategic advantage in Third World nations; and, further, that any resources released from cold war–related objectives have been directed toward relief of the budgetary problems of the rich countries rather than the development needs of the poorest. All of this is doubtless true. Beyond that, the successor states to the Soviet Union are not economically able to provide aid to developing countries, a category into which many of them now fall.

But it is also evident that governments are beginning to accept a measure of responsibility for human well-being and are coming to realize— if only slowly—that investment in removing the underlying causes of conflict, whether interstate or intrastate, is an investment in their own security. Western countries, for example, have been willing to make major financial outlays in the interest of social and political stability in Russia. The United States invested a substantial amount of money in UNITAF to alleviate a social crisis in Somalia notwithstanding its own budgetary problems (and its indebtedness to the United Nations). Still, it will take strong intellectual and political leadership to bring a wide public understanding of the commonality of interest in deterring conflict through peace-building measures that should now bind the countries of the world together. Secretary-General Kofi Annan has placed major emphasis on peace-building as a means of avoiding conflict in his millennium report *We the Peoples*[2] and his comprehensive report *Prevention of Armed Conflict.*[3]

The United Nations can fill an important leadership role by establishing as the goal of a new era of fundamentally changed international relations the construction of a foundation for lasting peace. This may not sound very different from long-articulated UN ideals. What is new is the opportunity to pursue this objective in a greatly changed environment and with a revised assessment of what is—or should be—possible. The UN secretary-general has begun to take the lead in developing, in cooperation with UN agencies and Member States, the concepts, programs, and new instrumentalities needed for progress toward this goal and in defining the complexities, difficulties, and likely setbacks that will be entailed.

POSTCONFLICT PEACE-BUILDING

In *An Agenda for Peace* Secretary-General Boutros Boutros-Ghali addressed only postconflict peace-building, defining it as "action to identify and support structures which will tend to strengthen and solidify peace in order to avoid a relapse into conflict."[4] He suggested that it might include disarming the previously warring parties and the restoration of order, repatriation of refugees, advisory and training support for security personnel, monitoring elections, advancing efforts to protect human rights, reforming or strengthening governmental institutions, and promoting formal and informal processes of political participation. These are realistic objectives that have since the end of the cold war been successfully realized in various instances. Notable examples are the preparation and monitoring of elections in Nicaragua, the repatriation of some 300,000 refugees in Cambodia, and the contribution to institution building in Namibia, Mozambique, East Timor, and Kosovo.

There are also examples of failure: in Haiti, where effectively monitored elections did not lead to stable democratic governments, and in Angola, where the collection of weapons was imperfect and free elections did not prevent the resumption of civil war. It should not be expected that such undertakings will always succeed in establishing a basis of sustainable peace. A concept that entails such a high degree of idealism needs to be leavened with a healthy appreciation of reality if disillusionment is to be avoided. As one assesses the value of peace-building, analysis of the causes of failures will be as important as analysis of success. The world media can be counted on for assistance in this regard. At the same time, failures should not be allowed to overshadow successes or invalidate the concept of postconflict peace-building.

PEACE-BUILDING IN ITS BROADER DIMENSIONS

When seen in a larger context than postconflict situations, peace-building assumes even broader dimensions. It encompasses all actions and programs that can contribute to the deterrence of conflict and the strengthening of international security. This statement immediately raises the question: What is meant today by international security? As has been noted earlier, when the United Nations Charter was signed, international security meant that countries would not be subject to external attack, or to the threat of attack. Now, with the increased interdependence of peoples as well as of states, and the transparency that brings instantaneous global awareness of all serious threats to human well-being, the common understanding of international security has changed and continues to evolve. To maintain international security can now be reasonably interpreted as connoting the protection of states and peoples from mortal harm. Therefore to build peace must include both action to promote friendly relations between states and the encouragement of a free and harmonious social environment within states. This concept is, indeed, wide reaching and, if accepted, indicates the broad dimensions of peace-building. Peace-building needs to be seen as having many components— blocks in an edifice that, like the great cathedrals, will take generations to build. Boutros-Ghali has suggested that peace-building should be viewed as the counterpart of preventive diplomacy, which seeks to avoid the breakdown of peaceful conditions. But peace-building must also be seen *as preventive diplomacy* in its largest form. It is intended both to remove the underlying causes of conflict and to prevent its recurrence should conflict break out. As Annan has stated, ". . . every step taken towards reducing poverty and achieving broad-based economic growth is a step toward conflict prevention."[5]

Peace-building measures can be undertaken to overcome political, economic, or social weaknesses in national, regional, and global societies. Such measures are foreseen in the first article of the UN Charter, in which a principal purpose of the United Nations is defined as achieving "international co-operation in solving international problems of an economic, social, cultural or humanitarian character, and in promoting respect for human rights and fundamental freedoms for all." At the end of the founding conference in San Francisco, U.S. Secretary of State Edward R. Stettinius Jr., sounding much like the UN secretary-general today, had the following to say:

> In the next twenty-five years the development of the economic and social foundations of peace will be of paramount importance. If the United Nations cooperates effectively toward an expanding world economy, better living conditions for all men and women, and closer understanding among peoples, they will have gone far toward eliminating in advance the causes of another world war. . . . If they fail, there will be instead widespread depressions and economic warfare, which would fatally undermine the world organization. *No provisions that can be written into the Charter will enable the Security Council to make the world secure from war if men and women have no security in their homes and in their jobs* [emphasis added].[6]

It can be said, then, that the UN system, encompassing its functional offices and specialized agencies, has been engaged in peace-building from the time of its establishment.

Inis Claude, in his insightful book *Swords into Plowshares,* refers to "the functional approach to peace," stating that functional activities "which flourish luxuriantly in the United Nations" are immediately and explicitly concerned with such values as prosperity, welfare, social justice, and the "good life." Functionalism, he states, "envisages its task in terms of the alteration of the subjective conditions of mankind. War is caused by the attitudes, habits of thought and feeling that are fostered by the state system. Functional organizations may, by focusing attention upon areas of common interest, build habits of cooperation which will equip human beings for the conduct of a system of international relations in which the expectation of constructive collaboration will replace that of sterile conflict as the dominant motif."[7] Claude thus interprets social progress as a way of encouraging cooperation between states that will contribute to peace between them. This was clearly in the minds of the drafters of the Charter and of Secretary of State Stettinius in stressing the importance for peace of international cooperation in dealing with economic, social, and humanitarian problems. They were not thinking, however, of internal—intrastate—conflict.

Today, as we consider peace-building, it is especially desirable to examine what can be achieved by functionalism in removing the causes of internal conflict. This is where functionalism—social and economic development, humanitarian assistance, institution building—has its greatest relevance, as intrastate conflict has primarily societal roots. The relationship between social justice and peace is becoming more evident and more pressing.

It is increasingly accepted, albeit conditionally at times, that intrastate conflict, if it threatens unconscionable loss of life and property, is of legitimate concern to the United Nations. Governments were for the most part loath to become involved in the genocidal conflict that engulfed Rwanda in 1994 but since have come to see that this was a grave error.

Economic development, democratization, and protection of human rights or any of the other components of peace-building that have been mentioned are important objectives in themselves. But to view them as more than that, as elements with which to build a solid foundation for peace, provides an additional goal against which UN programs and program implementation can be assessed. Peace-building can provide a framework within which the central United Nations Organization, through the strength of its mandate for the maintenance of peace and international security, can exercise authoritative leadership in the UN system as a whole. This can do much to bring about the close coordination among the functional agencies acting in accordance with agreed priorities that, until now, has been impossible to achieve.

PEACE-BUILDING IN ACTION

Given the very breadth of peace-building, it is useful to identify spe-cific measures in order to lend reality to the concept and appreciate what the United Nations has done and might do in the future. It is hardly contestable that extreme poverty, accompanied as it usually is by mal-nutrition, disease, underemployment, and high birth rates, can—and too often has—contributed to social upheavals that, in turn, have led to armed domestic conflict. Many of the extensive programs initiated within the UN system over the years to promote economic development have eased these problems and thereby contributed to building a foundation for peace. But a good many—even while engendering economic growth—have not brought a notable reduction in the social and political tensions within the recipient countries. This may in some circumstances be unavoidable. More could be accomplished, however, if the various requirements for peace-building in the particular social and political circumstances of a targeted country or region are factored into the design and implemen-tation of economic development projects and if projects of the various functional agencies and bilateral donors are coordinated with this purpose in mind.

As an example of such an approach, it is possible to think of a project for energy development in a country of varied ethnic or tribal compo-sition. The energy project would be desirable per se for the economic development of the country. It could, however, have either a positive or negative effect on the country's social cohesion. If the project is so de-signed as to benefit primarily one group within the country's population, the results in terms of peace-building could quite possibly be negative. If, on the other hand, the project is so designed as to involve potentially conflicting population elements in its planning and implementation, and if the energy produced can be seen as of common benefit, there can be a positive, complementary gain for political and social harmony as well as economic development within the country, an objective worth achiev-ing even if the cost of the project is thereby increased. In simple terms, economic development projects should, whenever practicable, tie the vari-ous social and political elements in a country into a network of practical cooperation and common interests.

Similarly, a complex of development projects within a region can serve to build peace among several countries if it is planned by the various UN and regional agencies, together with bilateral donors, so as to link the countries in a web of mutual economic interest and cooperative en-deavor. The Mekong River project, in which Laos, Cambodia, Thailand,

and Vietnam are cooperating to develop the Mekong River basin, shows the potential of this approach. An integrated plan for the equitable utilization of the water resources of the Middle East (on which several agencies have worked) could have a major postconflict peace-building impact if political circumstances ever permit its implementation.

Peace-building is more tangible when seen in the shorter-range perspective of evident nascent crises stemming from economic or social causes within a country or region. In such circumstances the element of threat, with political as well as economic and social implications, is likely to be clear. Programs can be designed to alleviate the specific threat and resources mobilized for their realization. Again, to cite an illustrative, theoretical example: Friction between two ethnic groups in one of the poorer South Asian countries is intensified because a prolonged drought has caused great hardship among the ethnic group most heavily engaged in farming and resulted in a large influx of this group into the cities where the other ethnic group has been traditionally dominant. Riots ensue and the stability of the government is threatened. Carefully focused assistance programs are required to alleviate the hunger, encourage resettlement, and strengthen respect for human rights if they are under threat.

This requires the same kind of systemwide coordination as longer-term assistance programs, but, given the more evident humanitarian and international security implications, the UN secretary-general is in a stronger position to take the lead in organizing coordinated action to counter the threat. The secretary-general can bring the situation to the attention of the General Assembly (and, if the security threat is imminent, to that of the Security Council) in the expectation that the assembly will call on agencies and governments to cooperate in a program to be organized by him. In such circumstances the lead can be taken by the secretary-general either through his designation of a special representative to organize the systemwide provision of the needed assistance or through his designation of a lead agency to carry out this function in the understanding that the agency will have the continuing advice of the Secretariat staff.

Such a procedure is not without precedent. At the time of the African Sahel famine in the 1980s Secretary-General Javier Pérez de Cuéllar appointed a senior member of his staff to mobilize support from Member States and coordinate bilateral and multilateral emergency programs. This effort was largely successful once it got under way even though a centrally important specialized agency, the Food and Agriculture Organization, proceeded largely on its own. The UN action should have begun earlier, however, which illustrates a further need for deterrent peace-building: early warning. As was stated in chapter 2 of this book, there is no structure through which information from the various sources within the UN system can be systematically synthesized for purposes of deterrent peace-building and preventive diplomacy. Secretary-General Boutros-Ghali suggested in his 1992 *Report on the Work of the Organization* that the United Nations should possess an "early warning function able to detect threats to security and well-being from energy crises to the burden of debt, from the risk of famine to the spread of disease."[8] Secretary-General Annan, as part of his major reform program to reduce duplication of efforts and facilitate greater complementarity and coherence, reorganized the Secretariat's work around the UN's five core missions: peace and security, economic and social affairs, development cooperation, humanitarian affairs, and human rights. Four executive committees were established to oversee the first four of these areas, with human rights included in the mandate of each. As a result of this restructuring, the secretary-general is better able to foresee where and in what form peace-building measures are needed. Rational utilization of resources available to the United Nations has been improved. The needed resources, however, remain woefully inaccessible.[9]

SOCIAL DEVELOPMENT AS PEACE-BUILDING

Like economic assistance programs, social development programs constitute an essential element in peace-building. Such social objectives as the reduction of disease, the growth of literacy, population management, and protection of the environment are so evidently linked to the development of stable societies that the introduction of the concept of political peace-building objectives in long-term planning is scarcely necessary. The priority areas for implementation of a program for the elimination of malaria, for example, will obviously be determined by the prevalence of the disease. But seeing such programs as relevant to strengthening international security can provide additional justification for the larger resources that are needed.

In the shorter term, where social tension threatens to reach critical proportions, the need to focus social development efforts specifically to reduce the likelihood of conflict becomes more evident. If abuse of human rights becomes widespread in a country, efforts to improve the situation are a needed element in peace-building. The problem that is likely long to remain for the United Nations is how to do this while respecting national sovereignty as provided in the UN Charter. As suggested earlier in a different context, one guideline should be that if a government requests assistance in strengthening respect for human rights within its territory, then action by the United Nations to do so cannot infringe its sovereignty or contravene the provisions of Article 2, paragraph 7, of the Charter. Even if there is no request (and one cannot be elicited) the UN Human Rights Commission can, at the request of another state, review the situation and send a fact-finding mission or rapporteur to investigate the situation (although entry to the country would be dependent on the willingness of the government to issue visas). Such public exposure, even if on-the-spot investigation is not possible, can serve to encourage restraint on the part of the authorities and improve the prospects of peace within the society. If the abuse of human rights reaches the point where it can be justifiably considered as conflict threatening international security, stronger measures may be required. In such an eventuality the stage of peace-building would be passed and the stage of forceful intervention under Chapter VII of the Charter reached.

In his 1991 Annual Report to the General Assembly, Secretary-General Pérez de Cuéllar wrote, "I believe that the protection of human rights has now become one of the keystones of the arch of Peace." And, further, "the case for not impinging on the sovereignty, territorial integrity and political independence of States is indubitably strong. But it would only be weakened if it were to carry the implication that sovereignty, even in this day and age, includes the right of mass slaughter or the launching of systematic campaigns of decimation or forced exodus of civilian populations in the name of controlling civil strife and insurrection."[10] Each of Pérez de Cuéllar's successors has expressed the same opinion.

DEMOCRACY AND PEACE

A constant political element in peace-building is the encouragement of freedom and the strengthening of democratic forms of government. In UN constitutional terms this is justified by the determination expressed in the UN Charter to promote social progress and better standards of life in freedom. It is also in substantive consonance with the mandate of the United Nations to preserve peace because the course of history, at least since the wars associated with the American and French revolutions, suggests that democratic governments tend not to wage war on other democratic governments.[11] The UN was unable to pursue this objective effectively for most of its history because of the contradictory interpretations among Member States of what freedom and democratic government mean. Still, today, the practice of democratic government remains far from universal. But democracy as an *ideology,* meaning government formed on the basis of free elections and operating under the rule of law and respect for human rights, is now widely accepted *in principle,* with the evident exception of China and the few other remaining communist governments such as Cuba and North Korea. There is a clear majority of Member States in favor of assistance by the UN in the holding of free elections, as evidenced by the recommendation made by the General Assembly that a special unit be established in the Secretariat to provide such service.[12] In 1992 alone, the United Nations provided technical assistance for elections in Albania, the Congo, El Salvador, Ethiopia, Guinea, Guyana, Liberia, Madagascar, Mali, Rwanda, Togo, and Angola. In Central America, Namibia, Cambodia, East Timor, and Kosovo the UN has done more than monitor elections or provide technical advice. By helping to provide a stable national environment and security for elections in Nicaragua; by contributing to the drafting of the constitution in Namibia; by participating in implementation of the plan for a free, democratic government for Cambodia; and by assuming administering responsibilities in Kosovo and East Timor, the UN has been building a basis for peace *within* those countries or territories. As Boutros-Ghali stated in *An Agenda for Peace,* "There is an obvious connection between democratic practices—such as the rule of law and transparency in decision making—and the achievement of true peace and security in any new and stable political order. These elements of good governance need to be promoted at all levels of international and national political communities."

This type of political peace-building has until now been carried out largely in postconflict situations. However, as suggested in chapter 3 on peace-keeping, the UN should be in a position to assist Member States in the strengthening of democratic processes, on their request, in circumstances of internal tension prior to its escalation to armed combat. This is a prime example of a peace-building measure that the United Nations can now take—albeit with much discretion—that was not possible during the cold war period.

THE ROLE OF ECOSOC

Peace-building clearly calls for greater coordination of program planning and resource application not only among UN functional agencies, but also among national donors of bilateral aid. There needs to be an integrated approach to the objectives of peace, democracy, and human rights and the requirements of development.[13] The United Nations, as an institution, needs to be in a stronger position to give strategic direction to both multilateral and bilateral assistance programs. Further, a system needs to be developed through which the political and social dimensions can be more fully reflected in economic planning.

In principle, the Economic and Social Council (ECOSOC) should be the lead UN organ in dealing with peace-building. ECOSOC, which now consists of fifty-four Member States, may, according to the UN Charter, coordinate the activities of the specialized agencies through consultation with, and recommendations to, such agencies and through recommendations to the General Assembly and to the members of the United Nations. Moreover, "It may make arrangements with the Members of the United Nations and with the specialized agencies to obtain reports on the steps taken to give effect to its own recommendations and to recommendations on matters falling within its competence made by the General Assembly."[14] Thus ECOSOC is endowed with the threefold responsibility of policy formulation, program coordination, and monitoring of policy implementation. These responsibilities are of central importance to the success of the United Nations in building peace. But lacking any real source of power or authority in the formulation of global policies, ECOSOC was largely ineffective during most of the UN's history. Only in the past decade has its operation improved and its reputation grown, if only marginally.

In 1991 the decision was made that ECOSOC would have only one substantive session annually instead of two, as had been the case until then. This was intended as part of the restructuring and revitalization process of the United Nations in the economic, social, and related fields that inter alia would enable ECOSOC to enhance "its role as a central forum for major economic, social and related issues and policies and for coordinating functions related to the United Nations system." A specific objective is to pursue "an integrated approach to policy and programme aspects of the economic and social issues."[15] At its 1992 substantive session, ECOSOC declared that objectives of securing peace, development, and justice were indivisible and equally essential. The council reiterated that international development cooperation and the eradication of poverty were inextricably linked with the preservation of peace.

With only one annual session, greater discipline is required in formulating the agenda. Four or five days of each session are devoted "to the coordination of the policies and activities of the specialized agencies, organs, organizations and bodies of the United Nations system relating to the achievement of the economic and social objectives of the United Nations." The annual session now includes a "high level segment" of four days with ministerial participation as well as the participation of the heads of the relevant UN functional agencies and offices.[16]

Secretary-General Boutros-Ghali recognized that ECOSOC could hardly provide effective, continuing coordination of UN programs in the economic and social fields that are vital for peace-building if it was not in session for the greater part of the year. He therefore suggested, in addressing the high-level segment in 1992, that "a flexible high-level intersessional mechanism" be introduced "in order to facilitate a timely response to evolving socio-economic realities." Such a mechanism, he said, "would enable the Council to play a central monitoring and surveillance role within the United Nations."[17] Some such standing body competent to deal with economic and social problems affecting international security on a continuing basis would certainly enhance ECOSOC's role in peace-building. Governments did not respond, however, to the secretary-general's recommendation.

Secretary-General Annan proposed the establishment of a humanitarian affairs segment in ECOSOC. This was approved by the General Assembly, thus better equipping ECOSOC to deal with an essential element in peace-building. In the Secretariat, support for ECOSOC has been consolidated with all economic and social programs in one department. This has given ECOSOC the advantage of support personnel who are more knowledgeable and closely tied into the various economic and social activities of the United Nations that ECOSOC is supposed to coordinate. With all this, ECOSOC's influence on the peace-building process remains tenuous for a number of reasons.

First of all, unlike the Security Council's, decisions of ECOSOC only have the force of recommendations. They are not mandatory. No government has to follow an ECOSOC resolution even though, as is often the case, its representative may have voted for it. Second, ECOSOC has no resources at its disposal. It can recommend that other UN agencies provide assistance where there is need, but it cannot force them to do so. Third, ECOSOC's influence on the specialized agencies of the UN system, which control a substantial part of the resources that are available for peace-building and sustainable development, is minimal. The specialized agencies operate as independent entities, with their own funding and governing bodies. The secretary-general of the United Nations has no authority over them and no control over their programs. The UN system Chief Executives Board for Coordination (CEB) is responsible for facilitating cooperation and coordination among the agencies and functional UN programs.[18] The secretary-general serves as permanent chairman, thus assuming the status of primus inter pares, but this does not translate into any power beyond that of persuasion. The CEB includes the heads of all specialized agencies and functional programs of the UN system.

There is a long-standing understanding between the United Nations and the World Bank that the UN will not make recommendations to the bank on loans. It is sound policy that World Bank loans should not be subject to majority decision by the General Assembly. This should not exclude, however, close consultation between the United Nations and the financial institutions in the establishment of priorities and the design of programs that are intended to build a foundation for peace in a particular country. If economic structural reform programs and programs to strengthen democratic institutions are pursued by separate UN agencies without integration at the planning stage, their common objective of enhancing human security and building peace can be seriously jeopardized. This was unfortunately the case in El Salvador. Alvaro de Soto, the UN Mediator in the Salvadoran peace process, and Graciana del Castillo, a Secretariat economic officer, have written that "the IMF and the World Bank did not involve the United Nations in the elaboration of the economic stabilization *cum* structural adjustment programme. Similarly, when the United Nations became engaged in the negotiating process in 1990, it did not consult the IMF or the Bank, notwithstanding the serious financial implications that it would entail. . . . The United Nations, the IMF and the Bank did not operate as if they formed part of the same system, but rather as if they were functioning in separate worlds."[19] A good bit has been learned from this experience and from similar ones elsewhere. An effort is now being made to preclude such uncoordinated approaches to building peace, but problems still recur.

There has never been in the United Nations an effective means of synthesizing the programs of the functional offices and agencies in pursuit of commonly agreed priority objectives determined on the basis of political as well as economic and social considerations. For peace-building purposes, greater cooperation and integration of programs is needed. The most direct way of achieving this might seem to be to centralize control of program formulation of the specialized agencies, including the financial institutions, in the UN General Assembly, with the UN secretary-general accorded supervisory status over the heads of these agencies. But this would run directly counter to the intentions of the founders of the organization.

Centralization of control was deliberately avoided as giving the central UN organization too much power and as permitting political disputes, with which the General Assembly and the Security Council would inevitably be concerned, to disrupt the work of the functional agencies. Moreover, it was considered that the central UN organs would not have the expertise or the time to deal with the technical subjects with which the functional agencies would be concerned. These considerations are still valid. The General Assembly is not well suited to exercise supervisory control over the specialized agencies. Moreover, any such plan would encounter such strong opposition from the specialized agencies and from Member States as to render it unworkable. Nonetheless, greater guidance from the central UN organization, which is concerned with political as well as social and economic factors, is needed for peacebuilding. An invigorated ECOSOC, if it enjoys the greater authority that can come from the commitment of Member States, could meet this need at least in part, without requiring a change in the Charter or departing from its original intent. Acting under instructions from ECOSOC, the secretary-general could serve as its agent in exercising a degree of supervision over the specialized agencies.

However, the steps taken are patently far from sufficient to enable ECOSOC to give central leadership and direction for either the policy formulation or program integration needed for peace-building. It is worth noting that the General Assembly resolution that defines the changes made in ECOSOC speaks only of the revitalization of the United Nations in the economic, social, and related fields. No mention is made of international security in this context, or of peace-building.

It remains the case that the authority that ECOSOC needs to play a lead role in peace-building will depend on the following conditions:

- The willingness of Member States to regard it as the principal forum for global policy formulation;
- The readiness of Member States, as members of the specialized agencies, including the financial institutions, to accord ECOSOC clear responsibility to coordinate the programs of the system;
- The ability of the secretary-general or the senior Secretariat officials in the economic and social areas to provide intellectual stimulus in the formulation of global policies;
- The success of the structural reform that Annan has introduced in the economic and social areas of the United Nations;
- Development of a close working relationship between ECOSOC and the Security Council that will recognize the direct relationship between economic and social developments and international security.

For his part, Secretary-General Annan has exercised commendable leadership in the CEB and had some success in winning greater cooperation in common planning from specialized agency heads. Through structural reforms, he has synthesized the work of UN functional offices and programs in pursuit of commonly agreed priority objectives, determined on the basis of political as well as economic and social considerations. In line with his objective of systemwide coordination, he has brought into his office a staff of experts capable of interdisciplinary analysis to advise him inter alia on desirable action by agencies of the UN system as a whole for peace-building.

THE COMPETENCE OF THE SECURITY COUNCIL

Under the UN Charter, the Security Council is given primary responsibility for the maintenance of peace and international security. This has been interpreted until now as a political responsibility. The council has never dealt with economic and social issues per se, although it has determined that humanitarian crises can constitute a threat to international security warranting enforcement action under Chapter VII of the UN Charter. ECOSOC reports to the General Assembly, not to the Security Council. Because economic and social developments increasingly influence the maintenance of international security, the question inevitably arises as to the degree—if at all—that the mandate of the Security Council extends to these fields. How can the Security Council meet its responsibility to prevent war if it has no control or influence on social and economic developments? At least a partial answer is provided in the Charter, which states that ECOSOC may furnish information to and "shall assist the Security Council on its request."[20] It was thus foreseen from the beginning that the Security Council might, in pursuit of its mandate, interest itself in economic and social matters. This the council has not done so far. But it will need to do so if conflict is to be avoided in the coming years.

For this purpose, the Security Council and ECOSOC should develop a procedure for liaison and orderly consultation that takes into account their mutual objective of maintaining international security and building peace and their respective capacities to act. With regard to the latter, there is a distinctive difference between the Security Council and ECOSOC. Under Article 25 of the Charter, Member States commit themselves to accept and carry out the decisions of the Security Council. Its decisions relating to the maintenance of international security and peace are therefore binding in principle on all UN members. ECOSOC may only make recommendations. This it can do to the General Assembly, to Member States, and to the specialized agencies. It is reasonable to expect ECOSOC to take security considerations into account in recommending

policies and actions to the appropriate governmental and/or nongovernmental actors with the objective of building peace and to be responsible
for coordinating and monitoring their implementation. The Security Council, in turn, should have knowledge of, and take into account, economic
and social developments in determining action to be taken to maintain
and strengthen international security. The Security Council should have
responsibility to take *enforcement* action pertaining to such developments
should they constitute a threat to international security. Just as it has
called on a government to desist from an action such as massive violation
of human rights amounting to genocide, it could impose sanctions in the
event of noncompliance with treaty obligations governing protection of
the global environment. Secretary-General Boutros-Ghali suggested that
the secretary-general and the human rights bodies be empowered to bring
massive violations of human rights to the attention of the Security Council with recommendations for action.[21]

To recapitulate, peace-building is an undertaking that must engage at
some stage all parts of the United Nations system as well as governments
and regional and nongovernmental organizations. In such a broad en-
deavor effective leadership is of paramount importance. The United Nations is the only organization with a mandate broad enough for this role.
Secretary-General Boutros-Ghali made an energetic, sometimes abrasive,
effort to exercise such leadership, both personally and as chief administrative officer of the United Nations. Secretary-General Annan has taken
a more conciliatory and restrained approach that has brought better results. Progress has been made. To endow the United Nations with the
necessary leadership capacity for peace-building, however, a more fundamental reform of the economic and social sectors of the UN system
than has yet been undertaken will be needed. Only through such a process can ECOSOC and the secretary-general gain the authority to establish the policies and priorities that will guide the relevant activities of
all of the functional offices and agencies of the system. Resources available to the UN system will never be adequate to allow the luxury of
duplication. This means greater central direction and with it the ability
to ensure that resources available within the UN system and in national
and regional sources serve ultimately to strengthen the basis for peace
through the process of peace-building.

Fundamental reform of this nature will be strongly resisted by the
executive heads of some, if not all, functional agencies. It can only be
effected if Member States, who, after all, exercise control over the agencies, exert the necessary pressure. The countries of the North and the
South will have to work together in greater appreciation of the mutuality

of their interests. It may just be that the urgency of peace-building in the era of a threatening growth in global population, the prevalence of terrorism, and spiraling demands on global resources will persuade them to do so.

NOTES

1. See Immanuel Kant, "Eternal Peace," in *The Philosophy of Kant* (New York: Modern Library, 1949) for consideration of the relationship between "republican" government and peace.

2. Kofi A. Annan, *We the Peoples: The Role of the United Nations in the 21st Century* (New York: United Nations, 2000), chapters 1 and 3.

3. Kofi A. Annan, *Prevention of Armed Conflict,* UN document A/55/985-S/2001/574 (2001). Also available in book form published in New York by the United Nations in 2002.

4. Boutros Boutros-Ghali, *An Agenda for Peace* (New York: United Nations, 1995), p. 61.

5. Annan, *We the Peoples,* p. 45.

6. Edward R. Stettinius Jr., *Report to the President on the San Francisco Conference,* Department of State, 26 June 1945.

7. Inis L. Claude Jr., *Swords into Plowshares* (New York: Random House, 1984), chapter 17, pp. 378, 382.

8. UN document A/47/1, 11 September 1993, par. 71.

9. Kofi A. Annan, *Renewing the United Nations: A Programme for Reform,* UN document A/51/950 (1997), part I, par. 28.

10. Javier Pérez de Cuéllar, *Anarchy or Order* (New York: United Nations, 1991), pp. 341–42.

11. See Bruce Russett, *Grasping the Democratic Peace* (Princeton, N.J.: Princeton University Press, 1993).

12. See A/RES/46/137 (1991).

13. Ibid., par. 67.

14. UN Charter, Articles 63 and 64.

15. A/RES/45/264 (1991).

16. Ibid.

17. *Report of the Secretary-General on the Work of the Organization,* UN document A/47/1 (1992), p. 22.

18. The CEB was formerly known as the Administrative Committee on Coordination (ACC).

19. Alvaro de Soto and Graciana del Castillo, "Obstacles to Peacekeeping," *Foreign Policy* (Spring 1994), pp. 69–83.

20. UN Charter, Article 65.

21. UN document A/47/1, 11 September 1992, par. 101.

Chapter 6

TERRORISM AND WEAPONS OF MASS DESTRUCTION

Since its earliest days, the United Nations has sought to control the manufacture and use of weapons of mass destruction (WMD). It has never ceased to do so. Initially the focus was on atomic weapons because the world had just witnessed their infernal power in the bombs that fell on Hiroshima and Nagasaki. There was, however, an awareness from the beginning of other forms of such weapons. In 1948 the UN Commission for Conventional Armaments defined weapons of mass destruction as being "atomic explosive weapons, radioactive material weapons, lethal chemical and biological weapons and any weapons developed in the future which have characteristics comparable in destructive effect to those of the atomic bomb and other weapons mentioned above."[1] More than half a century later, this definition needs no change. The United Nations has actively dealt with each of the identified categories separately under the general heading of disarmament measures and with them all together in its efforts to eliminate Iraqi WMD in the years since the end of the Gulf War. There have been notable achievements with regard to each category and in the case of Iraq's WMD capability. Although not all relevant agreements have been accomplished within the UN framework, they have without exception had the UN's strong support and endorsement.

Terrorism has also long been on the UN's agenda but dealt with, like weapons of mass destruction, in terms of its various elements rather than a generic whole. This changed dramatically following the terrorist attacks in the United States on September 11, 2001. Suddenly, terrorism in general came to the fore as a global threat and was addressed as such (albeit without an agreed definition) in both the Security Council and the General Assembly and by the secretary-general. In the context of terrorism, the threat of weapons of mass destruction became more imminent. The two threats of terrorism and weapons of mass destruction converged, each intensifying the other. The challenge posed for the United Nations was daunting, demanding departure from long-established traditions and the tackling of the highly divisive issues of intervention, the gathering of intelligence, and the definition of terrorism.

NUCLEAR WEAPONS

In its first resolution, adopted on January 24, 1946, the General Assembly called for the elimination of "atomic weapons and other weapons capable of mass destruction." In this same session, the assembly established the Atomic Energy Commission. Its purposes were the elimination of atomic weapons from national armaments (with effective safeguards through inspections) and the promotion of the use of atomic energy for peaceful purposes. The United States introduced the co-called Baruch plan, which called for a multilateral atomic development authority that would control all potentially dangerous atomic activities, foster the use of atomic energy for peaceful purposes, and, to this end, carry out a program for research and development. The United States proposed to destroy its nuclear weapons and turn over its nuclear supplies to the multilateral authority once the authority was established. The plan was unacceptable to the Soviet Union and was eventually abandoned. However, the UN's concern to limit and ultimately eliminate nuclear weapons has continued to the present day.

Treaties and agreements that relate to the limitation or reduction of U.S. and Soviet/Russian Federation nuclear weapons, such as SALT I, SALT II, and the ABM treaty were negotiated between the two powers without UN involvement. However, two treaties have been negotiated and signed within the framework of the United Nations that are of great significance—real in one case and potential in the other—on the development and proliferation of nuclear weapons. The first is the Treaty on the Non-Proliferation of Nuclear Weapons (NPT), which entered into force in 1970. The treaty represents a bargain according to which those states without nuclear weapons agree not to acquire them, and those states with nuclear weapons agree not to provide the material for making nuclear weapons to nonnuclear states and eventually to eliminate their own nuclear arsenals. Under safeguards agreements, which are provided for in the treaty, the International Atomic Energy Agency (IAEA) conducts inspections of peaceful nuclear installations to ensure that nuclear fuel is not being diverted for military use.

Review conferences are held every five years under the auspices of the United Nations to assess progress or the lack thereof in implementation of the NPT. The record is both good and bad. Only one signatory state, North Korea, has withdrawn from the treaty. Argentina, Brazil, and South Africa, all of which had the technical capacity "to go nuclear" and for many years declined to sign the treaty, are now members. (South Africa, under the apartheid regime, had begun a secret nuclear weapons program, which it publicly abandoned when the Mandela government took office.) With South Africa's adherence, only three states remained nonsignatories that had the technical capacity and the suspected ambition to possess a strategic nuclear capacity: India, Pakistan, and Israel. Both India and Pakistan have now tested nuclear weapons and thus joined the nuclear club. Israel is widely believed to have long had a nuclear capacity, something Israel's government will neither confirm nor deny. Thus, while the number of parties to the treaty has increased to 187 as of 2003, the number of avowed nuclear powers has increased by two, with Israel and now North Korea ever more evidently falling into this category. Iraq, a treaty party, sought to produce a nuclear weapon in contravention of its treaty commitments. Iran has also been accused of having this goal. Equally negative in the view of a large majority of treaty parties is the failure of the five original nuclear signatories of the NPT—the United States, the United Kingdom, Russia (the USSR), France, and China—to move further toward meeting their commitment under the treaty eventually to eliminate all their nuclear weapons. They, in turn, point to the significant reductions that are being made in strategic nuclear warheads by the United States, Russia, and, to a lesser extent, by the United Kingdom and France.

The Complete Test Ban Treaty (CTBT) is the second treaty directly related to the development and proliferation of nuclear weapons that has been negotiated and signed within the framework of the United Nations. In the early 1960s, the United States, the United Kingdom, and the Soviet Union reached agreement on a treaty banning nuclear tests in the atmosphere, outer space, and underwater. The three powers signed the Partial Test Ban Treaty in October 1963 and opened it for signature by other states. The treaty has remained in effect ever since and has been supplemented by a further bilateral agreement between the United States and the Soviet Union limiting the power of underground test explosions. The more ambitious objective of a complete ban on nuclear testing was on the agenda of the UN's Committee on Disarmament before the three powers completed the Partial Test Ban Treaty. It languished there until January 1994, when serious substantive negotiations on a treaty began in an ad hoc committee established for this purpose. After more than two years of intensive negotiations, the treaty was completed. On September 10, 1996, the General Assembly adopted the Comprehensive Nuclear-Test-Ban Treaty and requested the secretary-general to open it for signature at the earliest possible date. By mid-2003 the treaty had been signed by 167 countries and ratified by 102. But there was, and remains, a problem. According to Article XIV of the treaty, forty-four named states must ratify the treaty before it can come into effect. Among these countries are North Korea, Pakistan, and India, who have not signed the treaty, and the United States, which signed the treaty only to have the U.S. Senate reject ratification. So while a commission has been formed to prepare for the implementation of the treaty, the prospects of its coming into effect are cloudy at best.

NUCLEAR-FREE AREAS

One of the most effective steps taken to limit the spread of weapons of mass destruction is the exclusion of nuclear weapons from large areas of the earth's surface and from outer space. The following treaties and agreements are at present in force.[2] All were negotiated with the strong support of the United Nations, some within the framework of the organization and some outside of it.

Antarctica. The Antarctic Treaty was adopted in 1959, demilitarizing an entire continent and creating the first nuclear-free zone. It prohibits the testing of any kind of weapon and the disposal of nuclear waste on the continent.

Outer Space. The Outer Space Treaty of 1967 prohibited military maneuvers and the placing of nuclear and other weapons of mass destruction in earth orbit and on celestial bodies, including the moon. China and other members of the Committee on Disarmament have proposed that the prevention of an arms race in outer space be placed on the committee's agenda. This proposal has not been accepted.

Latin America and the Caribbean. The Treaty of Tlatelolco, which established Latin America and the Caribbean as the first inhabited nuclear-free region, was opened for signature in 1967. Each country and territory became bound by the treaty on ratification by its governing authority.

The Deep Sea Bed. The 1971 Sea Bed Treaty prohibits the placement of nuclear weapons on or under the ocean floor beyond a twelve-mile limit of the coastline.

The South Pacific. The Treaty of Rarotongo, which entered into force in 1986, established the entire South Pacific as a nuclear-free zone.

Southeast Asia. The Bangkok Treaty, which established Southeast Asia as a nuclear-free zone, entered into force in 1997.

Africa. The Treaty of Pelindaba, establishing the African Nuclear-Weapon-Free Zone, was agreed upon in 1996 but will come into effect only when twenty-eight countries have ratified it. As of 2002, this had not yet happened.

OTHER WEAPONS OF MASS DESTRUCTION

All known categories of weapons of mass destruction, other than nuclear weapons, have been prohibited by multilateral treaties negotiated within the United Nations. The following are the principal treaties.

Chemical Weapons

The Geneva Protocol of 1925, to which almost all countries are now party, prohibited the use of bacteriological weapons and asphyxiating, poisonous, or other gases in war. The protocol said nothing about the manufacture or storage of such weapons, which a good many countries continued to do even after signing it, thus giving rise to the reasonable apprehension that the protocol was an insufficient means to ensure that such weapons would never be used. The UN Committee on Disarmament therefore undertook to prepare a treaty that would constitute a comprehensive ban on chemical weapons. After ten years of often frustrating negotiations, the committee reached agreement in 1992 on the Chemical Weapons Convention (CWC) on the Prohibition of the Development, Production, Stockpiling and Use of Chemical Weapons and on Their Destruction.[3] This convention is the first multilateral agreement that provides for the elimination of an entire category of weapons of mass destruction. The system of verification that it entails is unprecedented. The CWC came into effect in April 1997. More than 140 states are party to the convention, including the five Permanent Members of the Security Council.

Biological Weapons

The Convention on the Prohibition of the Development, Production and Stockpiling of Bacteriological (Biological) and Toxin Weapons entered into force in March 1975, supplementing the 1925 Geneva Protocol on the same subject.[4] As of mid-2003 there were 147 parties to the convention. The absence of any formal verification regime to monitor compliance has limited its effectiveness. (Iraq, which during the Saddam Hussein regime is known to have produced and stockpiled bacteriological weapons, is a party to the convention.) An Ad Hoc Group was established in 1994 to develop a legally binding system of verification but has not achieved its goal, not least because the United States is fearful that such a regime would offer opportunities for industrial espionage.

Radiological Weapons

Weapons using radiological material were included among the potential weapons of mass destruction in the definition given in the list developed by the 1948 Commission for Conventional Armaments to which reference was made earlier. The United States and the Soviet Union submitted a joint proposal to the Committee on Disarmament in 1979, but other states introduced considerations such as the risk of mass destruction from radioactive substances disseminated as a result of military attacks on civilian nuclear power installations. As a result, while numerous declarations have been made against the use of radiological weapons, no convention has been completed. Fortunately, as of yet no radiological weapons of mass destruction have been created.

Modification of the Environment

In light of the use of defoliants by the United States in Vietnam and wide concern over possible melting of the polar icecaps for military purposes by nuclear explosions, a Convention on the Prohibition of Military and Other Hostile Use of Environmental Modification Techniques was agreed upon in the Committee on Disarmament. It came into effect in 1978. Under the convention, states undertake not to engage in "military or any other hostile use of environmental modification techniques having widespread, long-lasting or severe effects as the means of destruction, damage or injury to any other State Party." An environmental modification technique is defined as "any technique for changing—through deliberate manipulation of natural processes—the dynamics, composition or structure of the earth, including its biota, lithosphere, hydrosphere and atmosphere, or of outer space."[5]

Other Possible Weapons of Mass Destruction

In 1979 the Soviet Union submitted a list of potential weapons of mass destruction to the Committee on Disarmament. In addition to radiological weapons, it included particle-beam weapons, infrasonic acoustic radiation weapons, and electromagnetic weapons operating at certain radio frequency radiations that could have injurious effects on human organs. Western countries at the time expressed a readiness to work out agreements on specific types of weapons should they emerge but argued that a single treaty covering all potential new weapons of mass destruction would have to be so general and vague as to be neither effective nor verifiable. No agreement has ever been drafted, and none of these potential weapons has become operational. Conventions prohibiting or restricting the use of certain conventional weapons that may be deemed to be excessively injurious or to have indiscriminate effects and the Ottawa Convention on Anti-Personnel Land Mines have been drafted and agreed to in the United Nations forum and are in effect. They are not considered in detail here because they do not fall within the category of weapons of mass destruction. However, it is worth noting that since the anti-personnel land mine treaty came into effect, the number of those killed or maimed in such trouble spots as Afghanistan, Bosnia, Cambodia, and Mozambique has decreased substantially. Fewer new mines are being laid and legal trade in the deadly weapons has come to a halt.[6]

THE SADDAM HUSSEIN EFFECT

Prior to the 1991 Gulf War, weapons of mass destruction appeared generally under control even though massive amounts of strategic nuclear warheads remained in the U.S. and Russian arsenals. Disarmament interest in the United Nations had begun to focus on conventional arms, especially land mines. Surprisingly, the proven use of chemical weapons by Saddam Hussein in the Iran/Iraq war and against Iraq's Kurdish citizens produced only a muted international outcry. However, at the time of the Gulf War, when the Coalition forces prepared to drive the Iraqi army out of Kuwait, there was much concern among Coalition military commanders that Iraq might use its known chemical weapons against them. There was also sufficient fear of Iraqi use of bacteriological weapons (the possession of which had not then been confirmed) to prompt extensive anthrax vaccination of U.S. troops. In a letter addressed to Hussein but delivered to Deputy Prime Minister Tariq Aziz, President George

Herbert Walker Bush warned that Iraq would suffer intolerable consequences if it used chemical weapons in the war. Saddam Hussein refrained from doing so.

When the war ended, the United Nations responded to the threat by establishing the UN Special Commission (UNSCOM) with the mandate to root out and destroy not just one or two specific types of weapons but to root out Iraq's *entire* weapons of mass destruction capacity, both existing and potential.[7] UNSCOM, using sensitive intelligence and highly intrusive inspections, discovered that Iraq had not only produced and weaponized large quantities of the most deadly chemical materials, it had also carried out extensive experimentation with bacteriological elements and had succeeded in weaponizing them, although their effectiveness in battle was untested. It was within a year of being able to manufacture a relatively primitive but highly destructive nuclear bomb. For delivery of these weapons, Iraq retained a number of Scud missiles, provided earlier by the Soviet Union, and an unknown number of domestically produced copies with a longer but probably less accurate range. UNSCOM destroyed the overwhelming majority of these weapons but was prevented by the Iraqis from completing its mission. It was unclear to what extent Iraq retained a chemical and bacteriological capacity, but it was obvious that it had the technical know-how to continue to develop these weapons. Once excluded from Iraq, UNSCOM was unable to maintain a monitoring system, as foreseen in the Security Council resolution, that would preclude Iraq from resuming its weapons of mass destruction program.[8]

In 1999 the Security Council dissolved UNSCOM because it could no longer hope to enjoy even the minimum Iraqi cooperation required for its work and because it had lost the confidence of important members of the Security Council. In its place the council established the United Nations Monitoring, Verification and Inspection Commission (UNMOVIC) which, together with the International Atomic Energy Agency (IAEA), was to complete the tasks that had been given to UNSCOM and the IAEA in Security Council resolution 687. Denied entry by the Iraqi regime for about two years, UNMOVIC and IAEA were able to resume inspections only after the United States threatened to invade Iraq unless it could be shown that Saddam Hussein had fully complied with the council's demand that Iraq relinquish all WMD and its capacity to build them. Concluding from the initial UNMOVIC and IAEA inspection reports that Iraq had not shown a credible intent to comply with the council's demands, the United Sates and the United Kingdom invaded Iraq on March 17, 2003, in order (according to them) to force him to do so. UNMOVIC and the IAEA were thus supplanted as the instruments for eliminating any remaining Iraqi WMD capacity.

The Iraqi experience forced the United Nations to confront an extremely difficult question: What can it do if a country fails to comply with treaty obligations regarding WMD or terrorism and thus constitutes a serious threat to international security? The Security Council's unprecedented answer in the case of Iraq was to prohibit the country from possessing any kind of WMD as well as related delivery systems and to impose comprehensive economic sanctions as a means of forcing it to comply. When, even under the pressure of the long-sustained sanctions, Iraq failed to account satisfactorily for the elimination of its WMD capacity a second question arose: Should the council authorize military action under Chapter VII of the Charter to remove WMD capacity in the hands of an irresponsible government? In the case of Iraq the response of the Security Council was ambiguous. Most members agreed that military action would be justified if and when the threat was proven to be real and beyond other remedy. That stage, they concluded had not been reached. A minority, including the United States, concluded that quick military action was essential to counter the threat by an Iraq controlled by Saddam Hussein in possession of WMD capacity. In 2003 the United States and the United Kingdom went to war with Iraq in this conviction without the explicit authorization of the Security Council.

These questions were again posed, albeit in less dramatic terms, when North Korea failed to comply with IAEA inspection requirements under a nuclear safeguards agreement to which it had adhered. As provided under the IAEA Statute, the IAEA informed the members of the Security Council of the failure of North Korea to comply with its obligations. The council adopted an admonitory resolution but otherwise did nothing, leaving it to the United States to attempt in bilateral negotiations to dissuade North Korea from pursuing any nuclear ambitions.

The success that this course produced proved short-lived. North Korea not only subsequently admitted that it had built a nuclear facility capable of contributing to the production of nuclear weapons; it thereafter proceeded to give notice of its withdrawal from the Nuclear Non-Proliferation Treaty. As this is written, the Security Council has not yet decided on an appropriate response. The imposition of economic sanctions against a country that is already suffering from widespread malnutrition would be counterproductive. Agreement in the council on military action under Chapter VII appears unlikely. Clearly the response given to the Iraqi possession of WMD does not provide a precedent for North Korea or other cases that may arise in the future.

Two other developments have added to the potential threat of weapons of mass destruction that the various treaties had sought to control. One was that with the collapse of the Soviet Union, the security of its nuclear weapons and nuclear material became questionable. The fear arose that nuclear fuel would, through theft or bribery, come into the possession of terrorist elements or rogue states. A second development was the emergence of India and Pakistan as nuclear powers. This did not contravene any treaty commitment because neither country had signed the NPT. However, it is doubtful whether either country has the advanced and expensive security systems to ensure the safety of their nuclear weapons. Moreover, governmental stability in Pakistan has been fragile, leaving open the possibility of a government takeover by Islamic militants or access to nuclear material by dissident elements.

In these circumstances, the dramatic and deadly emergence on September 11, 2001, of a terrorist network clearly prepared to use weapons of mass destruction confronted the United Nations as well as the wider international community with a grim challenge. Within the UN, only the Security Council had the authority and power to deal with it.

TERRORISM

When terrorism moved to the top of the international agenda with the devastating terrorist attacks against the United States, the United Nations reacted with unaccustomed swiftness. The secretary-general proclaimed that "the United Nations stands four-square against terrorism, no matter what end it purports to serve."[9] While the United Nations had never been able officially to define terrorism (and still has not), it had been concerned with its various attributes since the early 1960s, when a series of airliner hijackings took place. Beginning in 1963, the United Nations and its agencies developed twelve international legal conventions that provide a legal basis for the international community to take action to suppress terrorism and bring those responsible for it to justice. Instead of criminalizing terrorism as such, these conventions criminalize specific acts of terror. Signatories are obliged to ensure that their domestic law criminalizes the acts described in the conventions. When a suspected perpetrator of one of these acts is found on the territory of a signatory, that state has a legal obligation to extradite or prosecute the accused. Following are the twelve conventions.[10] They are all in effect, although the number of states party to the more recent conventions remains relatively small.

- *Convention on Offenses and Certain Other Acts Committed on Board Aircraft* (1963). This convention authorizes the airplane commander to impose reasonable measures on any person who has committed or is about to commit such acts and requires states party to take custody of offenders.

- *Convention for the Suppression of Unlawful Seizure of Aircraft* (1970). Under this convention states party are required to punish hijackings by "severe penalties" and either extradite or prosecute the offenders.

- *Convention for the Suppression of Unlawful Acts against the Safety of Civil Aviation* (1971). States party are required under this convention to punish offenses by "severe penalties" and either extradite or prosecute the offenders.

- *Convention on the Protection and Punishment of Crimes against Internationally Protected Persons, including Diplomatic Agents* (1973). States party agree under this convention to criminalize and punish attacks against state officials and representatives.

- *Convention against the Taking of Hostages* (1979). States party agree to make the taking of hostages punishable by appropriate penalties, to prohibit certain activities within their territories, to exchange information, and to carry out criminal or extradition procedures.

- *Convention on the Physical Protection of Nuclear Material* (1979). This convention obliges parties to ensure the protection of nuclear material during transportation within their territory or on board their ships or aircraft.

- *Convention for the Suppression of Unlawful Acts of Violence at Airports Serving International Civil Aviation* (1988). This convention extends the provisions of the other aviation-related conventions to airports.

- *Convention for the Suppression of Unlawful Acts against the Safety of Maritime Navigation* (1988). This convention obliges members either to extradite or to prosecute alleged offenders who have committed unlawful acts against ships such as seizing ships by force and placing bombs on board ships.

- *Protocol for the Suppression of Unlawful Acts against the Safety of Fixed Positions located on the Continental Shelf* (1988). This extends the requirements of the previous convention to fixed platforms such as those engaged in the exploitation of offshore gas and oil.

- *Convention on the Marking of Plastic Explosives for the Purpose of Detection* (1991). This agreement seeks to curb the use of unmarked and undetectable plastic explosives.

- *International Convention for the Suppression of Terrorist Bombings* (1998). Under this convention the parties seek to deny safe havens to persons wanted for terrorist bombings by obligating each government to prosecute such persons if it does not extradite them to another country.

- *International Convention for the Financing of Terrorism* (1999). This convention obligates states party either to prosecute or to extradite persons accused of funding terrorist activities and requires banks to enact measures to identify suspicious transactions.

In addition to these legally binding instruments, the General Assembly in 1994 adopted the Declaration on Measures to Eliminate International Terrorism,[11] which condemned all acts and practices of terrorism as criminal and unjustifiable, wherever and by whomever committed, and urged all states to take measures at the national and international levels to eliminate international terrorism.

These conventions clearly entail binding commitments by governments to take effective action against terrorism. But they provide a legal basis for action rather than prescribe an automatic enforcement response to violations. The Security Council must still decide the action to be taken or authorized. This is an especially critical point because governments remain free under these conventions to determine what distinguishes a terrorist act from an act of national liberation or self-determination. Even so, the General Assembly resolution and the later conventions show an acceptance that terrorism demands forceful countermeasures. Thus, following the adoption of the International Convention for the Suppression of Terrorist Bombings, the Security Council imposed sanctions against Libya to force it to hand over two persons accused of complicity in the bombing of a U.S. airliner over Lockerbie, Scotland. There was surprisingly little criticism and no condemning resolution in the General Assembly when the United States unilaterally bombed Osama bin Laden's training camps in Afghanistan and a chemical factory in Sudan after terrorist attacks on U.S. embassies in East Africa in 1998. After the September 11 terrorist acts most Member States seemed to agree with Secretary-General Kofi Annan when he said, " I understand the need for legal precision. But let me say frankly that there is also a need for moral clarity. There can be no acceptance of those who would seek to justify the deliberate taking of innocent life, regardless of cause or grievance. If there is one *universal* principle that *all* peoples can agree on, surely it is this."[12]

POST–SEPTEMBER 11 ACTIONS OF THE SECURITY COUNCIL AND THE GENERAL ASSEMBLY

In resolutions adopted prior to September 11, 2001, the Security Council had already unequivocally condemned all acts of terrorism as criminal

and unjustifiable and called on Member States to take specific measures
to prevent them.[13] It had also specifically demanded that the Taliban turn
over Osama bin Laden to appropriate authorities so that he could be
brought to justice.[14] But the September 11 attacks gave terrorism a new,
universally threatening dimension. Within twenty-four hours of the destruction of the Twin Towers in New York and the simultaneous attacks
in Washington, D.C., and Pennsylvania, the Security Council met and
approved an unprecedented resolution condemning such acts "like any
other act of international terrorism, as a threat to international peace and
security."[15] The unanimous approval included the votes of the council's
Muslim representatives, Bangladesh, Mali, and Tunisia. The resolution
called on "All States" to work together urgently to bring to justice the
perpetrators, organizers, and sponsors of these terrorist attacks and stressed
that all those responsible for aiding, supporting, or harboring the perpetrators, organizers, and sponsors of the acts "will be held accountable."
This resolution, which placed countering terrorism squarely under Chapter VII of the Charter, legitimized the use of force by Member States in
combating terrorism. It was followed on September 28 by resolution
1373,[16] which directly ordered Member States, inter alia:

- to prevent and suppress the financing of terrorist acts;
- to criminalize the willful provision or collection, by any means, directly
  or indirectly, of funds by their nationals or in their territory to carry out
  terrorist acts;
- to take the necessary steps to prevent the commission of terrorist acts,
  including the provision of early warning to other states;
- to ensure that terrorist acts are established as serious crimes in domestic
  laws and regulations; and
- to become parties as soon as possible to the relevant international conventions and protocols and fully implement them.

These are mandatory requirements placed on Member States by the Security Council, which expressed "its determination to take all necessary
steps in order to ensure the full implementation of this resolution." To
monitor implementation, the council established a high-level Counter-
Terrorism Committee of all members of the council. States are required
to report at regular intervals to the committee on the steps that they have
taken to comply.

The General Assembly on September 12 also adopted by unanimous
vote a resolution condemning the "heinous" acts of terrorism against the
United States. The assembly called for international cooperation "to pre-

vent and eradicate acts of terrorism," and stressed "that those responsible for aiding, supporting or harboring the perpetrators, organizers and sponsors of such acts will be held accountable."[17]

THE UN'S ROLE IN COMBATING TERRORISM

The United Nations is unlikely to deploy a UN force against terrorism. The support and resources for such action are lacking. The Counter-Terrorism Committee of the Security Council can press governments to take the actions mandated by the council but it cannot force them to do so. Most states have replied to the committee promptly, but many of the initial responses were too imprecise to provide assurance that the requirements of the resolution were being fully met. Moreover, some states lacked the legal authority or the resources to implement the required antiterrorism measures. Thus there are limits on what can be expected of the United Nations. Yet it can hardly be doubted that the remarkably quick and comprehensive action taken by the Security Council after the September 11 attacks, together with the earlier conventions and protocols that the United Nations had agreed, will assist substantially in the fight against terrorism. Significantly, no doubt was expressed on the legitimacy of the military action taken under U.S. leadership in Afghanistan against the Taliban and Al Qaeda. It was universally accepted because it was seen as authorized under Security Council resolutions.

Of equal importance, the United Nations can do much to eliminate some of the root causes of terrorism. Secretary-General Annan has emphasized that terrorism is "a weapon for alienated, desperate people, and often a product of despair. If human beings everywhere are given real hope of achieving self-respect and a decent life by peaceful methods, terrorists will become much harder to recruit."[18] Continued promotion of human rights, humanitarian assistance, and economic development can be a major UN contribution in eliminating terrorism. UN efforts to control the production of weapons of mass destruction that might fall into terrorist hands, as in the UNSCOM operation in Iraq, also fill a need. Similarly, UN action to eliminate illicit traffic in weapons, drugs, and other commodities such as diamonds can weaken terrorism by depriving terrorist groups of resources. Seen in this perspective, the role of the United Nations in combating terrorism is of critical importance despite the inability of Member States to agree on a generic definition of the term.

NOTES

1. Cited in United Nations, *Everyone's United Nations,* 10th ed. (New York: United Nations, 1986), p. 173.

2. The texts are available from http://www.un.org/Depts/dda/index

3. The text is contained in UN document A/RES/54/54E.

4. The text is available from http://www.un.org/Depts/dda/index

5. Ibid.

6. Of the five Permanent Members of the Security Council, only the United Kingdom and France are parties to the anti–personnel mine convention. However, the other Permanent Members comply with many of its provisions.

7. S/RES/687 (1991).

8. See Jean Krasno and James S. Sutterlin, *The United Nations and Iraq: Defanging the Viper* (Westport, Conn.: Greenwood, 2003) for a full account of the operations and achievements of UNSCOM.

9. UN document SG/SM/8105 (2002).

10. Texts of the conventions and the current number of states party to them are available from http://untreaty.un.org/English/Terrorism.asp

11. A/RES/49/60 (1994).

12. Text of Annan's speech available from http://www.un.org/terrorism/statements/sg.html

13. S/RES/1269 (1999).

14. S/RES/1267 (1999).

15. S/RES/1368 (2001).

16. S/RES/1373 (2001).

17. A/RES/56/1 (2002).

18. UN document SG/SM/8105, 18 January 2002.

Chapter 7

THE POTENTIAL OF REGIONAL ORGANIZATIONS

In speaking of the maintenance of international security, Winston Churchill once proclaimed that "There should be several regional councils, august, but subordinate; these should form the massive pillars upon which the world organization would be founded in majesty and calm."[1] This is perhaps the most flamboyant statement of that school of thought that attributed very high importance to the role of regional organizations in maintaining peace. At the San Francisco Conference, when the United Nations was founded, there was strong support for this approach. Those countries already committed to regional arrangements—the British Commonwealth, the Pan-American Union, the Arab League—insisted that adequate provision be made in the UN Charter for effective regional participation in the preservation of peace. The Latin Americans objected to the veto power of the Permanent Members of the Security Council on the ground that it could jeopardize the authority and cohesion of regional organizations. Australia, along with Belgium and Venezuela, proposed to qualify the veto in the case of regional enforcement action.[2]

The United States, pressed by the Latin American countries, supported recognition in the Charter of the role of regional organizations. At the same time, however, the Americans were wary of the regionalist approach, reflecting a continuing Wilsonian tendency to identify regionalism with competitive alliances. Secretary of State Edward Stettinius Jr. reported to President Harry Truman that concessions to regionalist pressures should not establish "a precedent which might engender rivalry between regional groups at the expense of world security."[3]

What emerged in the UN Charter is, as was necessary, a compromise. The Charter, according to Inis Claude, "conferred general approval upon existing and anticipated regional organizations, but contained provisions having the purpose of making them serve as adjuncts to the United Nations and subjecting them in considerable measure to the direction and control of the central organization."[4]

The course of history since San Francisco has led neither to regional organizations that would form pillars of the United Nations, in Churchill's phrase, nor to a United Nations intent on dominating or directing regional organizations for purposes of international security. But the United Nations has begun to work with them and even to rely on them. The cooperation between the United Nations and regional organizations on security problems was tenuous at best for most of the years since 1945. However, as the UN has assumed ever-greater responsibility in dealing with regional and internal conflicts in the post–cold war era, it has looked more to the regional organizations as partners or, in some case, its agents. There have been profound disappointments and many misunderstandings. As experience has grown, however, so too has realism as to what can be expected and what each can do best. Regional organizations, for their part, have recognized the need for the UN to be active—even dominant—in handling intrastate conflicts, especially in peacekeeping and peace-building.

The number and range of what are broadly referred to as regional organizations are very large. NATO, the Arab League, and the Caribbean Community (CARICOM) all can be categorized under this heading, although not necessarily as coming within the purview of Chapter VIII of the UN Charter, which defines the relationship between the United Nations and "regional arrangements." Regional organizations can be concerned primarily with economic cooperation, mutual security, political coordination, or a combination of these and other concerns. For our present purposes, regional arrangements can be defined as intergovernmental in nature—this is certainly the assumption of the Charter. A regional arrangement or organization, then, is an organization in which governments from a defined region or with a close connection to the region are joined for commonly agreed purposes.

The UN Charter is not concerned with all regional organizations; rather, only those dealing "with such matters relating to the maintenance of international peace and security as are appropriate for regional action." There is no objection to UN Member States joining such organizations provided "they are consistent with the Purposes and Principles of the United Nations."[5]

Most if not all of the regional organizations that fit into this category include some form of commitment to these purposes and principles in their charters. The North Atlantic Treaty, for example, commits its parties to conform to the rules of international behavior laid down in the UN Charter, provides that NATO activities will be conducted within the authorization and limitations prescribed in Article 51 of the Charter, and disavows any intent to revise the rights or duties of parties that are members of the United Nations or to infringe upon the established responsibilities of the Security Council.[6]

THE CONSTITUTIONAL RELATIONSHIP BETWEEN THE UN AND REGIONAL ORGANIZATIONS

Article 52 of the UN Charter suggests that local disputes should be settled in the first instance through regional arrangements "either at the initiative of the states concerned or by reference from the Security Council." The prerogative of the Security Council is preserved to investigate any dispute, as is the right of any state to bring a dispute directly to the council or the General Assembly. Article 53 of the Charter provides that no enforcement action is to be taken by a regional organization without the authorization of the Security Council, but the council "*shall where appropriate, utilize such regional arrangements or agencies for enforcement action under its authority*" (emphasis added). The council had never resorted to this until the conflict in the former Yugoslavia. In seeking to halt Bosnian Serb attacks on "safe areas," the council, as we have seen, decided that "Member States, acting nationally or through regional organizations or arrangements, may take . . . all necessary measures, through the use of air power, in and around the safe areas in the Republic of Bosnia and Herzegovina, to support UNPROFOR in the performance of its mandate." This mandate was "to deter attacks against the safe areas, to monitor the cease-fire, to promote the withdrawal of military and paramilitary units other than those of the Government of the Republic of Bosnia and Herzegovina and to occupy some key points on the ground, in addition to participating in the delivery of humanitarian relief. . . ."[7] The intent was to utilize NATO for enforcement purposes even though NATO was not named.

Formal agreements exist between the United Nations and a number of regional organizations including the Organization of African Unity, the League of Arab States, and the Organization of the Islamic Conference defining their relationship. The agreements with the regional organizations provide for cooperation in general terms, but they do not contain provisions governing the handling of regional disputes or the exchange of information relative to international security. An agreement was negotiated between the Organization of American States and the UN but has not been signed. The Conference on Security and Cooperation in Europe (now the Organization for Security and Cooperation in Europe, OSCE)[8] declared in 1992 that it was a regional arrangement within the meaning of Chapter VIII of the Charter. All of these organizations now have observer status with the UN, as does the European Union.

THE PERFORMANCE OF REGIONAL ORGANIZATIONS IN SECURITY MATTERS

From one perspective, the primarily internal nature of most regional conflicts would suggest that regional organizations are best suited to resolve them. The regional organizations should be more familiar with the root causes; their intervention would seem less "foreign"; their peace-keepers might seem more readily acceptable to the people involved if they shared a similar culture and language. On the basis of recent experience, however, rather the contrary is the case. The dominant role of the United Nations in dealing with most regional disputes is evident, for example in Western Sahara, Cambodia, the Persian Gulf, Afghanistan, Angola, Nicaragua, Haiti, Mozambique, Somalia, Rwanda, Sierra Leone, the Democratic Republic of the Congo, and, with significant exceptions, the former Yugoslavia. The only regional conflict situation that has been primarily handled by regional parties since the end of the cold war is the civil war in Liberia. Even there, the UN has been active through the application of sanctions. Given the continuing deterioration of the internal situation in Liberia, UN Secretary-General Annan has recommended the deployment of a UN peacekeeping force in cooperation with the Economic Community of West African States (ECOWAS) to provide security for the population and an opportunity to restore responsible governance in the country.

The Organization of American States

Of the regional organizations, only the Organization of American States (OAS) has had notable success in the resolution of regional disputes without the participation of the United Nations. These include conflicts between Costa Rica and Nicaragua (1948–49, 1955–56, 1959), Honduras and Nicaragua (1957), Venezuela and the Dominican Republic (1960–61), Venezuela and Cuba (1963–64, 1967), the Dominican Republic and Haiti (1950, 1963–65), Panama and the United States (1964), and El Salvador and Honduras (1960–70). These solo achievements ended more than a quarter of a century ago. This can be attributed to increased intrusion of the cold war into the region; declining homogeneity as a result of the admission of more English-speaking Caribbean countries; increased dissatisfaction with U.S. policy orientation and U.S. dominance of the organization; and, finally, the declining enthusiasm of the United States, itself, for the OAS. With the end of the cold war, the ideological tension within the region declined substantially, and the OAS, with encouragement from the United Nations, has become more engaged in dealing with regional conflicts. The OAS utilizes its Unit for the Promotion of Democracy for long-term conflict prevention planning.

The Association of Southeast Asian Nations

The Association of Southeast Asian Nations (ASEAN) was founded with the primary goal of assuring regional peace and security. Its members called for collective political defense to protect individual as well as group interests. The concept of military defense was intentionally avoided.[9] An ad hoc body of mediators was established as a legal mechanism for the peaceful settlement of disputes. ASEAN members are legally bound to seek its help before turning elsewhere for assistance in the event of a dispute. Members have so far not needed to make use of this facility. ASEAN aided in bringing the parties together to end the Cambodian conflict, working in coordination with the United Nations, which ultimately assumed the major role in the development and implementation of the peace plan for the country (greatly facilitated by the Permanent Members of the Security Council). ASEAN efforts on Cambodia brought greater political solidarity to the association and made of it a stronger regional organization with enhanced potential. ASEAN, however, did not have a role in the peace enforcement and peace-building involved in the transition of East Timor to independence. This was entirely in the hands of forces acting under a mandate from the UN Security Council or, for the peace-building process, of the United Nations as an organization.

The Organization of African Unity

In June 1983 the Organization of African Unity (OAU), "against the background of many prolonged and destructive conflicts on our continent and of our limited success at finding lasting solutions to them," estab-

lished the Mechanism for Conflict Prevention, Management and Resolution. The mechanism has as a primary objective the anticipation and
prevention of conflicts. In circumstances where conflicts have occurred,
its responsibility is to undertake peacemaking and peace-building functions. If conflicts "degenerate to the extent of requiring collective international intervention and policing, the assistance or, where appropriate,
the services of the United Nations will be sought."[10] In 1999 ECOWAS
established a similar mechanism.

Unfortunately, the efforts of the OAU at peacemaking and peacekeeping have been singularly unsuccessful. Its experience in Chad and Western Sahara demonstrated that alone it has neither the resources nor the
internal cohesion to undertake successfully peacemaking or peacekeeping
within the region. Significantly, it has played no role in the Liberian
conflict or in resolving the conflicts in southern Africa that preceded
Namibia's transition to independence and only a tangential role in Somalia and Sierra Leone.

When asked by the UN secretary-general to assume responsibility for
peacekeeping in Rwanda, the OAU declined on the ground that the
United Nations was better equipped to do it. The OAU is only able to
deploy small observer groups (as it did in Rwanda when the first peace
agreement was reached). Involvement in intrastate conflict also poses a
problem for the organization. The OAU secretary-general dealt with this
issue head-on when he addressed the first meeting of the Conflict Prevention Mechanism. Assuming that the OAU was prepared in principle
to intervene in such conflicts, he asked members to decide whether an
identical approach should be taken to all categories of internal conflict—
"those arising from the process of democratization, those that are eth-
nically based, or those that are religious in nature."[11] This question has
not been answered.

Islamic Organizations

The League of Arab States and the Organization of the Islamic Conference (OIC) have been no more successful than the OAU in dealing
with regional conflict. Both sought to resolve the Iran-Iraq war with no
success. The Arab Deterrent Force that was deployed in Lebanon in 1976
was not, strictly speaking, an Arab League undertaking (having been
initiated solely by Syria) and was in any event hardly a success. With
the Iraqi invasion of Kuwait, the league was not only impotent; it split
as a result of internal pressures, a repetition of its earlier experience at

the time of Egypt's peace with Israel. In response to the severe conflict that erupted between Israel and Palestinians in 2002, the League, at the initiative of Saudi Arabia, agreed on a proposal intended to bring peace to the Middle East. The proposal, which was based on the principle of "land for peace," called for withdrawal of Israel to its 1967 borders, the establishment of a Palestinian state with Jerusalem as its capital, recognition of Israel by all the Arab states, and satisfactory arrangements for the return or compensation of Palestinian refugees. Agreement on this proposal, representing a rare show of unanimity among the Arab states, suggests that the unrest in the Middle East sparked by the spread of militant Islamic fundamentalism has prompted greater cohesion among the Arab states. The League took a unified stand in opposition to the U.S.-led military action against Iraq in 2003 although several members provided facilities of various kinds for the United States and its partners. The Arab League remains a largely powerless organization.

The OIC is the second major Islamic organization. It includes fifty-six member states, which amounts to all states having a predominantly Muslim population. The OIC is intended inter alia to strengthen solidarity and cooperation among Islamic states and promote the peaceful settlement of disputes between them; to eliminate racial discrimination and all forms of colonialism; to support the Palestinian people; and to safeguard the holy places such as Mecca, Medina, and Jerusalem. The OIC has played no significant security role, and its membership is too varied to develop common political policies beyond those of the Non-Aligned Movement, with which it largely overlaps. It participated in the development of a failed peace plan for Somalia but was otherwise inactive in that conflict.

The Commonwealth of Independent States

The Commonwealth of Independent States (CIS), which incorporates twelve of the fifteen republics of the former Soviet Union, enjoys observer status at the United Nations as a regional arrangement under Chapter VIII of the Charter. It has undertaken peacekeeping actions in several of the new states that emerged from the disintegration of the Soviet Union. In Georgia the CIS engaged in joint action with the UN and the OSCE. However, the CIS peacekeeping forces are quite different from those organized by the UN because they are composed almost entirely of Russian troops and are commanded by Russian officers. They have been deployed only in countries in which Russia has so direct an interest as to raise questions concerning the impartiality of the CIS forces. Russia has requested that the United Nations endorse and provide financial support for the CIS peacekeeping operations. The UN so far has declined financial support but, after much hesitation, legitimized the CIS action in Georgia as falling within the mandate of the Security Council for peacekeeping in that country.

As a regional organization, the CIS is inevitably dominated by Russia. Russia contends that it bears special responsibility for the security of the former republics of the Soviet Union. In the words of Russian Foreign Minister Andre Kozyrev, "Russia cannot pull out of Abkhazia or Tajikistan the way America did from Somalia." He insisted that "Russia's peacekeeping mission . . . acts in complete accordance with international law and at the request of the states concerned. But the cooperation of the world community, including the use of international observers and material support, is of great value."[12] The CIS, until now, has only acted within the territory of the former Soviet Union. Because the CIS commanders and most of the troops are Russian, there remain doubts as to whether it is a true regional arrangement within the meaning of the Charter.

European Regional Organizations and the Yugoslav Crisis

There has been a wide inclination to think of the European Union (EU)[13] as the center of economic power in Europe, the OSCE as the arbiter of human and democratic rights, and NATO as the military guarantor of peace and stability in Europe. The events in Yugoslavia proved that while this neat categorization was not always valid, it fairly delineates until now the role that each can best perform in the face of internal ethnic strife in Europe that amounts to civil war.

The OSCE, the EU, NATO, and the Western European Union (WEU) all became engaged in efforts to end hostilities in the former Yugoslavia. This was the first time any of them had sought to end armed conflict in the interest of regional security, with the exception of a brief NATO effort to temper the hostility between Greece and Turkey over Cyprus. They are the best organized, the best equipped, and the best financed of all the regional organizations. Each has been shown to have a different role in dealing with conflict situations; these roles needed to be defined over a period of time and had to be fitted in—sometimes with difficulty—with the responsibilities undertaken by the United Nations. It is instructive, in this respect, to examine the operations of the UN and the European regional organizations in the former Yugoslavia.

The Organization on Cooperation and Security in Europe

The Organization on Cooperation and Security in Europe (OSCE) has, as its name implies, the mandate to encourage security and cooperation in all of Europe. Yugoslavia was a charter member. When Yugoslavia broke apart and conflict erupted, the OSCE (then the CSCE) seemed the most appropriate organization to step in, bring an end to the fighting, and work toward a resolution of this eminently European problem. It was quickly seized of the conflict and, almost as quickly, proved incapable of effective action. First, the OSCE functions on the basis of consensus and there was no consensus on the action it might take in Yugoslavia. Furthermore, it had no military force at its disposal and no experience in organizing one, so the deployment of troops for peacekeeping, fact-finding, or deterrent purposes was not an option even if decisions had been possible. Similarly, it lacked the authority to impose sanctions. The OSCE proved ineffective in preventing the conflict in Yugoslavia and was immobilized and dependent on other organizations to take action to end the violence. That changed when the conflict in Bosnia was brought to an end and the stage was reached when the peace-building process could begin. Under the Dayton Accords signed on November 21, 1995, the OSCE was given the leading role in the political dimensions of the peace-building process. It was charged specifically with preparing and supervising elections and seeing to it that the results were implemented; with disarmament and arms-control measures; and with promoting respect for human rights and the development of pluralistic and independent media. The last charge listed—the promotion of democratic processes, respect for human rights, and the rule of law—became the major responsibility of the OSCE in subsequent peace operations in Europe, most notably in Kosovo. Outside of the Yugoslav context the OSCE has achieved some success in preventing ethnic conflict through the work of its high commissioner on national minorities. The high commissioner is charged with the task of seeking early resolution of ethnic tensions that might endanger peace.

The European Union

In the face of the intensifying conflict that accompanied the disintegration of the former Yugoslavia, the European Union (still, then, the European Community) assumed for the first time a security role that entailed peacekeeping and peace enforcement measures as well as peacemaking and peace-building. It acted fairly promptly—first alone and then in conjunction with the UN—in an eventually futile attempt to assist the

Yugoslav states to find a new federal structure that would be satisfactory to all parties. It deployed unarmed civilian monitors in Croatia in an attempt to quell the violence. But the EU quickly encountered problems that seriously handicapped its efforts. First, it was not accepted by the Yugoslav parties as an impartial third party because various members were suspected of favoring either Croatia or Serbia. Germany publicly pushed for recognition of Croatia (and Slovenia) as independent states, which the Serbs viewed as a hostile attitude. Second, the EU, like the OSCE, did not have the capacity to field a credible peacekeeping force as a means of stabilizing the situation. The unarmed observers, whose only protection was distinctive white uniforms, were ineffective. The EU imposed mandatory sanctions on weapons shipments to the former Yugoslavia but these, too, were largely ineffective, being restricted in applicability to EU members. The UN Security Council subsequently imposed similar, and ultimately broader, sanctions that were universally applicable.

Since these first unsatisfactory experiences, EU members have agreed to follow a common foreign and security policy. In 1999 the EU Council placed conflict management at the core of the process of strengthening the EU's common security policy. It aims at having a capacity for autonomous action in responding to international crises "without prejudice to actions by NATO," including the deployment of 60,000 troops from national armies to contain conflict. It has defined four priority areas in developing a civilian crisis management capacity: police, strengthening of the rule of law, strengthening civilian administration, and civil protection.[14] The Policy Planning and Early Warning Unit of the EU serves as its focal point for conflict prevention and peace-building. The EU was initially mainly active in the humanitarian assistance and economic development aspects of conflict prevention and peace-building but in 2002 it assumed responsibility (from the UN) for providing civilian police to train and assist local police in Bosnia.

The Western European Union

The Western European Union, a largely dormant Western European military organization, was activated when conflict first broke out in the former Yugoslavia. The intention was to provide a military peacekeeping arm for the EU. Aside from deploying some ships to enforce the sanctions imposed by the EU, this proved to be a failure. There were no readily available troops, there was no command and control machinery in place, and, most importantly, the organization was unable to agree on the precise purpose for which a force would be deployed. The WEU again became largely dormant. The EU has referred vaguely to the eventual integration of the WEU's potential into the EU's security strategy, but specifics are lacking.

The North Atlantic Treaty Organization

The conflict in the former Yugoslavia brought NATO to play an entirely new role in European security. The North Atlantic Treaty Organization was organized and structured as a defense organization. At the time of its establishment, the founders agreed to omit any reference in its charter to Chapter VIII of the UN Charter lest NATO action might thereby become subject to veto by the Security Council. This understanding was embodied in agreed minutes of interpretation in which it was said that "It is the common understanding that the primary purpose of this Treaty is to provide for the collective self-defense of the Parties. . . . It is further understood that the Parties will, in their public statements, stress this primary purpose, recognized and preserved by Article 51 [of the UN Charter], rather than any specific connection with Chapter 8 or other Articles of the United Nations Charter."[15] NATO has no specific mandate for conflict resolution.

The disintegration of the Warsaw Pact and the Soviet Union inevitably affected NATO's orientation and caused a search for new missions. Peacekeeping emerged as one of these. But when the conflict in Yugoslavia broke out, it was generally considered unthinkable that NATO could play a role in bringing it under control. While NATO had adequate, well-trained, and well-equipped troops, there was a wide assumption that it had no mandate to use them outside the NATO area, as Yugoslavia clearly was. NATO's responsibility was to deal with threats to its members from *other states,* not to restore peace *within* non-member states. The NATO secretary-general, Manfred Woerner, had stated in a 1991 interview that the organization should be "the focal point of a new pan-European security structure" and that as an expanded defense community it would eventually put peacekeeping forces in places of ethnic or border unrest "from the Atlantic Ocean to the Ural Mountains."[16] But Woerner added that he was expressing his personal opinion because consensus had proven elusive. Prior to the Yugoslav crisis NATO had had no contact with the United Nations, and the cultures of the two organizations were seen as totally different—one dedicated to the art of war and the other to the art of peace.

The fact that within two years of the disintegration of Yugoslavia NATO had begun to assist in the enforcement of a UN arms embargo against the Yugoslav states, well outside NATO territory; that it had offered to provide peacekeeping forces for the CSCE (now OSCE); and that it was poised to send war planes against the Bosnian Serbs in behalf of the United Nations is indicative of how quickly and fundamentally events in Yugoslavia influenced NATO and UN thinking. When the United Nations proved incapable of providing security for the ethnic populations in Bosnia, Secretary-General Boutros Boutros-Ghali, with the approval of the Security Council, turned to NATO for assistance. NATO agreed, monitoring no-fly zones, bombing Serb installations to provide security for protected areas, and ultimately assuming responsibility for peace-keeping in Bosnia under the terms of the Dayton Accords. A pattern emerged. Where a strong, well-organized, and well-equipped military force was required to bring an end to violent conflict in Europe, NATO would be relied on for the necessary military action. The UN would retain responsibility, along with other regional organizations and NGOs, for the other aspects of peacemaking and peace-building. In Kosovo, NATO acted militarily without a request (or legitimization) from the UN. This did not prevent the UN from accepting primary responsibility for the civilian administration and democratization of Kosovo, while NATO, having defeated the forces allied with Serbian president Slobodan Milosevic, retained the military security responsibility of peace enforcement. Once involved, NATO proved to be far and away the most effective regional organization in ending conflict and providing the security in which the peace-building process could go forward. After a rocky start, cooperation in Bosnia and Kosovo between NATO and the UN proved feasible and productive.

Yet there are circumstances that can make the utilization of NATO troops in resolving regional conflicts problematic. NATO, like the OSCE, acts on the basis of consensus, which means that any member can prevent or delay deployment, as France did initially in the case of the former Yugoslavia. Command and control of NATO troops will always be in the hands of NATO rather than the Security Council or the UN secretary-general. There is no formal agreement defining the relationship between NATO and the United Nations. NATO maintains only a single liaison officer at UN headquarters in New York. The lack of a structured system for consultation between the two organizations is an obvious disadvantage when they are engaged together in a peace operation. The most important limitations on wider utilization by the UN of NATO military force are NATO's unwillingness, until now, to participate in operations outside of Europe and the likely reluctance of non-European countries to accept NATO intervention in their regions.

THE UN ADVANTAGE

What, then, can be concluded concerning the role of the United Nations in dealing with regional threats to security? What effective action can the UN take that regional organizations cannot? What can the UN do to support the efforts of the regional organizations in seeking to control and resolve intrastate conflict? Again an examination of the UN's role in the former Yugoslavia provides some answers to these questions.

The UN action in response to the Yugoslav conflict can be summarized as follows:

- "Concerned that continuation of the situation constitutes a threat to international peace and security,"[17] the Security Council expressed full support for the European efforts to end the conflict, thus giving legitimacy to the actions of the European regional organizations in accordance with Chapter VIII of the UN Charter.

- In response to the request of the Yugoslav parties, who did not trust the objectivity of the EU, the Security Council invited the secretary-general to offer his assistance, in consultation with the Government of Yugoslavia and the European organizations, to bring an end to hostilities in Yugoslavia.

- Acting under Chapter VII of the Charter, the Security Council embargoed the shipment of weapons and military equipment to Yugoslavia and imposed comprehensive sanctions against Serbia and Montenegro.

- A personal envoy of the UN secretary-general joined with the EU in efforts to mediate a Yugoslav settlement and to resolve the Bosnian conflict.

- The Security Council authorized first the deployment of a military observer mission and then a full-scale peacekeeping force to maintain the cease-fire agreement in Croatia achieved through UN mediation.

- The UN established a symbolic peacekeeping presence in Sarajevo in the hope of preventing the outbreak of conflict there. It then deployed a limited peacekeeping force to secure the airport for humanitarian deliveries and, with subsequent expansion, to provide security for the delivery of humanitarian assistance where needed in the country. It resorted ultimately to enforcement measures under Chapter VII of the UN Charter to implement this mandate and to afford protection—unsuccessfully—to designated safe areas.

- The UN carried out a major humanitarian relief program under the leadership of the UN High Commissioner for Refugees.

- The Security Council established a War Crimes Tribunal for Yugoslavia and a committee to identify the persons to be tried.

- The UN deployed a modest *deterrent* peacekeeping force in Macedonia at the request of the Macedonian government but without the consent of neighboring Serbia, the party being deterred.
- The UN established a Transitional Authority in Eastern Slavonia (UN-TAES) that governed this heavily Serb region of Croatia for two years.
- The UN assumed responsibility for the civil administration of Kosovo pending the establishment of democratic local government for the territory.

The UN action in Bosnia has been subject to wide criticism as ineffective and, in some respects, ill advised. The United Nations was unable to end the conflict or to prevent ethnic cleansing and genocide. The massacre committed by Serbian forces at Srebrenica in the presence of UN peacekeeping forces will remain a permanent blot on the UN's record. Still, the UN provided the following key elements that the regional organizations could not or would not undertake:

- the capacity to deploy a large peacekeeping force for humanitarian purposes under adequate, if imperfect, command and control;
- the authority to impose universally mandatory sanctions;
- the ability to mobilize global support for humanitarian assistance and to provide the machinery and leadership for a massive humanitarian program;
- the authority to legitimize the enforcement action taken by a regional organization under Chapter VII of the UN Charter; and
- the capability of putting in place the civilian staff needed to administer Kosovo and Eastern Slavonia.

The Yugoslav experience tested the capacity of the UN as well as of European regional organizations to deal with regional conflicts. They all learned important lessons and gained a better understanding of the roles that each could best play. The actions taken by the United Nations, for the most part by decision of the Security Council, were significant as constituting a new interpretation of Article 2, paragraph 7, of the UN Charter prohibiting intervention in domestic affairs of states. The Canadian secretary of state for external affairs spoke to this matter in the following terms: "The concept of sovereignty is, of course, fundamental to statehood. . . . But the concept of sovereignty must respect higher principles. The time has now passed when the wanton destruction of human life is a matter of purely internal consideration."[18] The Yugoslav permanent representative told the Security Council that the Yugoslav example "might identify the new concept of the United Nations."[19] One cannot yet assume that this concept will be applicable in all circumstances. Only a week after these statements were made, the council was unable to adopt a resolution regarding a military coup in Haiti with its attendant loss of life because of concern on the part of some members that this would constitute interference in Haiti's internal affairs. The Security Council did not intervene effectively to prevent the genocide in Rwanda. Nonetheless, the Yugoslav experience demonstrated that the UN can take action in internal conflict situations, that this may require the application of force under Chapter VII of the Charter, and that the UN can, if necessary, request a regional organization to undertake enforcement action on its behalf.

The Macedonian request for the deployment of a UN peacekeeping force in order to *deter* a possible Serbian attack also tested a previously established limit on UN action. As noted in chapter 4, Secretary-General Boutros-Ghali recommended in *An Agenda for Peace* that the possibility be considered of the deterrent deployment of peacekeepers with the consent of only one party to a conflict. The Security Council had not responded to this recommendation at the time of the Macedonian request. It nonetheless acted favorably on the secretary-general's proposal that a deterrent force be sent to Macedonia. Thus the admissibility of this action was established by action rather than by a decision on principle. The action gave reassurance to Macedonia and may have prevented a Serbian intrusion.

In the former Yugoslavia, the OSCE and the EU both assumed wider responsibilities for democratization and protection of human rights, and NATO for the first time undertook extensive military peace enforcement operations. The mandate of the United Nations extends to all of these areas. The possibility for overlap and confusion was therefore substantial. However, by the time of the Kosovo operation the roles of the organizations had been defined in a way that worked and could stand as a flexible model in subsequent crises. In brief, if the application of well-trained, heavily armed military force was needed to enforce and maintain peace under perilous circumstances, the task could best be undertaken by NATO or, in non-European conflicts such as East Timor, by a strong regional coalition acting in lieu of a regional organization. Postconflict civil administration can best be the responsibility of the UN although the United States has been reluctant to accept this conclusion in the occupation of Iraq. The OSCE can concentrate on encouraging the growth of democracy through free elections and protection of human rights, while the EU can devote itself to such fields as refugee resettlement and economic development that are heavily dependent on resources.

The collaboration of regional organizations and the UN in post–cold war conflicts in other areas has been greatly influenced by the lack of other regional organizations as well endowed as those in Europe. In Central America peacekeeping could only be done by the United Nations, albeit with participation of troops from the region. Mediation responsibilities were shared by the UN and the OAS except in El Salvador, where the UN acted alone. In Somalia the UN provided the required peacekeeping and peace enforcement operations (in part by authorizing the United States to lead a military action on its behalf). It served as the principal mediator, in cooperation with the League of Arab States, the OAU, and the OIC, in seeking, unsuccessfully, an end to the fighting and national reconciliation. What is striking is the inability of the regional organizations, acting alone, to handle conflicts in their regions. The capacity to impose effective sanctions is limited, as shown by the experience of the EU in the former Yugoslavia and of the OAS in Haiti, where nonmember countries did not comply. Their ability to undertake peacekeeping operations is severely limited either by a lack of resources, as in the OAU, or by a lack of common will, as in the OAS.

COOPERATION BETWEEN THE UN AND REGIONAL ORGANIZATIONS

In *An Agenda for Peace,* Secretary-General Boutros-Ghali suggested that the design of cooperative work between regional organizations and the United Nations must adapt to the realities of each case with flexibility and creativity. As has been shown, the present capabilities and future potential of the various organizations vary greatly. In every case, however, a good bit can be gained from closer working contact between the organizations and the UN and from the development of a network among them for continuing exchange of information and mutual support.

Peacekeeping and preventive diplomacy are two fields related to international security in which enhanced and structured cooperation between the UN and regional organizations can be especially productive. The United Nations has amassed much valuable experience in peacekeeping and in such elements of peace-building as election monitoring, institution building, and protection of human rights. By sharing this experience through training programs, the UN can hasten the day when regional organizations can assume a greater share of the burden and do so effectively. Peacekeeping training afforded by the United Nations could cover not only the preparation of national troops for participation in UN peacekeeping or peace enforcement operations, but also the preparation of regional organizations to undertake peacekeeping operations themselves. The OAU and the OAS are now at a stage where they could profit from such assistance. The UN could profit, in reverse, from assistance from NATO in strengthening its command and control capacity. Consultations of a purely exploratory nature could be initiated with the League of Arab States while recognizing that its peacekeeping potential is likely to remain limited for a good time to come.

Since 1994 the United Nations and regional organizations have instituted a practice of holding biennial meetings for consultation and the exchange of information. Secretary-General Annan states in his report *Prevention of Armed Conflict,* written in 2001, that "meaningful progress has taken place with regard to coordination and consultation, better flows of information, visits of staff at the working level between the different headquarters, joint training of staff and joint expert meetings on specific cases for conflict prevention."[20]

The OSCE experience has shown that regional organizations are well suited to introduce various kinds of confidence-building measures. In the UN a number of studies have been completed on confidence-building measures that could be of benefit to those regions other than Europe where little has so far been done. Introduction of this subject into the consultative process can permit representatives of the various regional organizations to exchange experiences, review needs, and consider areas of potential mutual assistance.

It is not yet clear to what extent the early warning and conflict prevention capability of the United Nations will be strengthened through these exchanges because expertise at the regional level remains limited. But the regular consultations should in any event constitute an educational process for the regional organizations. As the constitutions continue, they can encourage greater transparency within the regions and greater mutual confidence among the regional states. They offer the potential additional benefit of nurturing a deeper sense of democratic participation by regional organizations in the maintenance of global peace.

Despite such favorable developments, there is little likelihood that regional organizations outside of Europe will, in the near future, be able to relieve the United Nations of very much of the burden it now bears in dealing with regional conflict. ECOWAS has demonstrated the capacity to deploy a peacekeeping force in Western Africa, but only under the dominating influence of Nigeria. It proved unable to control the internal conflict in Sierra Leone without the intervention of the UN and, briefly, the United Kingdom. The conflict prevention mechanisms that have been established by the OAU and the OAS have so far not shown great promise. Only the OSCE has had some success in dampening tensions before conflict erupts.

A serious lacuna inevitably exists in cooperation between the United Nations and regional organizations owing to the absence of such organizations in the regions where tensions are greatest and conflict is an ever-present threat: the North Pacific, South Asia, and, because the Arab League excludes Israel, the Middle East. This does not mean that enhanced cooperation between the existing regional security organizations and the UN is any less important. There is a realistic prospect that, in time, the European organizations and the OAS can undertake independent peacekeeping operations without encumbering UN resources. All of the organizations have a potential for confidence building (including regional arms limitation planning) and conflict prevention. The United Nations will become a stronger force for peace if it persists in efforts for a mutually productive relationship with the regional groups on the basis of a realistic assessment of the potential that each organization offers.

NOTES

1. Speech in The Hague, 7 May 1948; cited in Inis L. Claude Jr., *Swords into Plowshares* (New York: Random House, 1984), p. 113.

2. For a description of regional criticism of the veto see Ruth B. Russell, *A History of the United Nations Charter* (Washington, D.C.: Brookings, 1958), pp. 734–37.

3. Edward T. Stettinius Jr., *Report to the President on the San Francisco Conference* (Washington, D.C.: Department of State, 1945).

4. Inis L. Claude Jr., *Swords into Plowshares* (New York: Random House, 1984), p. 114.

5. UN Charter, Article 52.

6. The North Atlantic Treaty, preamble and articles 1, 5, and 7.

7. S/RES/836 (1993).

8. The Conference on Security and Cooperation in Europe (CSCE) was renamed the Organization for Cooperation and Security in Europe (OSCE) in 1993. OSCE is used in all later references to the organization.

9. For a statement of ASEAN purposes and principles see "Overview, Association of South-East Asian Nations," at http://www.aseansec./org/64, pp. 1–2.

10. *Declaration of Heads of State and Government*, Twenty-ninth Ordinary Session, 28–30 June 1993; OAU document AHG/Decl.3 (XXIX) Rev. 1.

11. Statement of the secretary-general of the OAU, Dr. Salim Ahmed Salim, to the inaugural meeting of the Control Organ at OAU Headquarters, 13 September 1993, in OAU press release of that date.

12. Andre Kozyrev, "The Lagging Partnership," *Foreign Affairs,* May–June, 1994, p. 68.

13. Until 1 January 1994, what is now the European Union (EU) was known as the European Community (EC).

14. "Common Foreign Security Policy/European Security and Defense Policy," Section III, p. 2. From http://ue.eu.int/pesc/pres.asp?lang = en

15. Cited in Dick A. Leurdijk, "Before and after Dayton: NATO in the Former Yugoslavia," *Third World Quarterly* 18 (1997), chapter 3, p. 4.

16. Quoted in the *Washington Post*, 4 October 1991.

17. S/RES/713 (1991).

18. UN document S/23076, 25 September 1991.

19. UN press release SC/5309, 25 September 1991.

20. Kofi A. Annan, *Prevention of Armed Conflict* (New York: United Nations, 2002), p. 74.

Chapter 8

THE POWERS AND RESPONSIBILITIES OF THE UN SECRETARY-GENERAL

The greatly increased international security activities of the United Nations that began in 1987 and have grown ever since have placed an unprecedented burden on the staff and structure of the organization, beginning inevitably with the secretary-general. The first secretary-general, Trygve Lie, described the job as the most difficult in the world. It has become even more demanding as the responsibilities of the United Nations for peacekeeping and peacemaking, for resolving conflict and providing humanitarian assistance, have grown exponentially without equivalent growth (or improvement) in the resources on which the secretary-general can call. The former U.S. attorney-general, Dick Thornburgh, in a report submitted to the secretary-general in March 1993 on relinquishing the post of under-secretary-general for administration and management in the Secretariat, stated that the United Nations Organization "today truly stands at a crossroads as to whether or not it can effectively adapt to these changing times. . . . The new responsibilities being assumed by the United Nations have raised the stakes and heightened the consequences in terms of human suffering should the United Nations fail to accomplish [its] new goals."[1]

The position of the secretary-general is somewhat analogous to that of chief executive officer of a transnational corporation. The principal undertakings of "UN Inc." relate to peace, economic and social development, and the various aspects of human security. Its board of directors is composed of practically every government in the world, a few of whom own the majority of the stock and are therefore more influential than the others. The position of secretary-general is described in the UN Charter as that of chief administrative officer, and not much more is said about it. Yet the managerial and diplomatic skills, the political acumen, and the talent for persuasion of this individual can influence substantially the success or failure of the United Nations in meeting the new and expanded tasks that have been described in the preceding chapters.

As a specially designated group in the U.S. Department of State was developing plans during World War II for a new international organization that would become the United Nations, the importance of the administrative function of its executive head (then usually referred to as "general secretary" or "director-general" and sometimes even as "president") was recognized. Not much attention was given to defining it, however, because it was assumed that administration of the new organization would follow the pattern already set in the League of Nations. Primary attention was given instead to the addition of a political dimension to the position. There was even the thought of having the "director-general" chair the meetings of the Security Council. In the end the political function was encapsulated primarily in Article 99, which authorizes the secretary-general to bring to the attention of the Security Council any development that, in his opinion, may threaten the maintenance of international peace and security. But most of the other responsibilities assigned to him (or, eventually, her) also inevitably entail a political dimension—even the formulation of the UN budget.

Because the secretary-general, under Article 97 of the Charter, acts as chief administrative officer "in all meetings of the General Assembly, of the Security Council, and of the Trusteeship Council, and shall perform such other functions as are entrusted to him by these organs," his responsibilities extend to the economic and social activities of the United Nations as well as the political and administrative. The secretary-general must be concerned with the entire agenda of the United Nations from human rights to the environment, from peace making to humanitarian assistance programs, from disarmament to illegal trafficking in drugs. The utilization in the Charter of the term "chief administrative officer" to describe the functions of the secretary-general is, if taken literally, misleading. The responsibilities inherent in the post can be best understood as falling under two headings: managerial and substantive. The two are in competition for the secretary-general's time and attention, with the substantive almost always winning.

The wisdom of combining potentially expansive political functions with responsibility for the administration of the organization was questioned on grounds of efficiency even as the plans for the United Nations were still at an early stage of development. But it was expected that the administrative aspects of the position, which were considered less important, could be "delegated,"[2] leaving the head of the Secretariat free to concentrate primarily on political and other substantive functions. This thinking continued through the Dumbarton Oaks and San Francisco Conferences. On neither occasion was any particular attention given to defining what the administrative responsibilities of the secretary-general would be or how they should be performed. This is partly accounted for by the expectation that there would be four or five deputy secretaries-general, elected in the same manner as the secretary-general, with the authority that election would convey. One elected deputy would have been responsible for administration. This idea was rejected in the end, notwithstanding the strong support of the Soviet Union, on the ground that it would compromise the independence of the Secretariat if the deputies to the secretary-general were dependent on the votes of governments for their jobs. More than fifty years passed before the General Assembly, in 1997, established the post of deputy-secretary-general. In accordance with the assembly's decision, the incumbent is not elected by the membership but appointed by the secretary-general. Kofi Annan appointed a Canadian diplomat and government minister, Louise Frechette, as the first deputy-secretary-general in 1998. Until then, the secretary-general did not have a deputy with full authority to manage the organization, and even now the deputy-secretary-general's authority does not approach that of the secretary-general because only the secretary-general enjoys the status of an elected official. The League of Nations administrative model was quickly overtaken. The United Nations, as an administrative structure, developed into a very different animal from the League of Nations so that what had worked there did not provide an adequate guide for UN procedures or management.

ASSESSING A SECRETARY-GENERAL'S PERFORMANCE

A number of states have been highly critical of political actions taken by a secretary-general. The Soviet Union, for example, sharply attacked the actions of Trygve Lie in connection with the Korean War and of Dag Hammarskjöld for his management of the Congo crisis. A number of Western countries were also unhappy in connection with the latter case as they were over the withdrawal by U Thant of the United Nations Emergency Peace-keeping Force (UNEF) from the Sinai in 1967. Indeed, the Soviet Union refused in the Security Council to concur in recommending the election of Lie for a second term, and it withdrew recognition of Hammarskjöld as secretary-general, motivated in both cases by dissatisfaction with political actions. Israel has frequently accused secretaries-general of lacking impartiality on the Middle East. But aside from these relatively few instances, the secretary-general has been routinely commended for his political actions. When there has been criticism in the political field it has often been for administrative weaknesses that have jeopardized political effectiveness, hardly ever for political judgment or lack thereof or for inadequacy as a mediator. There have been repeated calls for more effective preventive diplomacy. But here, too, emphasis has been on strengthening the administrative structure to provide the support needed for early warning and a global watch to make preventive diplomacy more feasible. Only with the advent of the extremely difficult questions regarding the use by the United Nations of military force in internal crises and the election of an outspoken, strong-willed secretary-general, Boutros Boutros-Ghali, was the political—or political/military—judgment of the secretary-general subjected to sharp criticism. This largely ended with the advent of Annan as secretary-general. The situation has been comparable in the other areas of the secretary-general's substantive competence as well. The United Nations has been subjected to almost constant criticism from Member States for inadequate leadership in economic affairs and, until recently at least, in such an important social field as human rights. But the criticism has seldom been directed at the secretary-general except, again, for administrative weakness in failing to produce an effective organizational structure and ensure adequate coordination within the UN system. This is something that Annan, on assuming office, set out to improve. He was not the first to do so but he has had more—albeit still limited—success than his predecessors.

THE IMPACT OF POST–COLD WAR DEVELOPMENTS

The political functions of the secretary-general have acquired greater prominence as a result of the new activism of the Security Council and of the increased, and sometimes controversial, involvement of the United Nations in intrastate conflict. This has direct implications for his managerial function. As the demands on the UN for peacekeeping, peace-building, humanitarian assistance, and other activities of high political sensitivity have escalated in the post–cold war years, the management

aspects of the position have become more demanding and more politically charged. To cite an illustrative example: As noted in an earlier
chapter, the General Assembly and the Security Council have both called
for an enhancement of the UN's preventive diplomacy and early-warning
capacity. The majority of members insist at the same time on a near to
no-growth budget. In his administrative capacity, the secretary-general
must somehow find the necessary resources or risk failure on the part of
the UN to carry out these preventive functions in a time when failure
can no longer be attributed to the effects of the cold war. Governments
expect a secretary-general to have the management skills of an outstanding corporate executive along with the political ability on which the
effectiveness of the UN in the maintenance of international security so
heavily depends. With a competent deputy-secretary-general on board
and with extensive reforms in place, Annan and future secretaries-general
may come closer to meeting these expectations than has been the case
in the past.

THE ORGANIZATION

The Preparatory Commission of the United Nations, having much in
mind the League pattern, developed a structure for the Secretariat that
consisted of eight departments, each headed by an assistant-secretary-
general:

- Security Council Affairs
- Economic Affairs
- Social Affairs
- Trusteeship and Non-Self-Governing Territories
- Public Information
- Legal Counsel
- Administrative and Financial Services
- Conference and General Services

In approving this plan, the General Assembly authorized the secretary-
general to "make such changes in the initial structure as may be required
to the end that the most effective distribution of responsibilities and
functions among the units of the Secretariat may be achieved."[3] Taking
advantage of this authorization, each secretary-general (and a good many
Member States as well) has sought to achieve a more effective distribution
of responsibilities and functions. New departments have been established

only to be subsequently eliminated. Functions have been transferred or consolidated. A Department of Peace-keeping Affairs has been added. But to an extent that is surprising in light of the growth in size and responsibilities of the United Nations, the structure devised by the Preparatory Commission for the Secretariat has remained fundamentally intact. The boxes on the charts have been rearranged, renamed, and grown more numerous. But were he to come back today, Lie would recognize the central elements of the Secretariat as he organized it. The major changes have been in size, from a Secretariat staff of 2,450 to one of more than 14,000,[4] and in the addition of numerous functional offices and programs spread widely over the world dealing with economic and social problems.

Thus, in addition to New York, there are three "headquarters" cities—Geneva, Vienna, and Nairobi—each of which is the location of functional offices such as the Office of the High Commissioner for Refugees (Geneva), the UN Environmental Program (Nairobi), and various offices related to the control of narcotic drugs (Vienna). There are also five regional economic commissions, located in Santiago, Geneva, Addis Ababa, Bangkok, and Amman.[5] All of these organizations, like the United Nations Development Program (UNDP), the Fund for Population Activities, and the United Nations Children's Fund (UNICEF) in New York, fall in principle within the managerial responsibility of the secretary-general. However, those that are supported largely by voluntary contributions and have their own governing boards; for example UNICEF, UNDP, and the Office of the High Commissioner for Refugees, are largely independent and responsible for their own administration and policies. In Bosnia, where the Office of the High Commissioner for Refugees was given overall responsibility for humanitarian assistance, the high commissioner, on at least one occasion, decided to withdraw personnel from areas under Bosnian Serb attack without consulting the secretary-general and, it turned out, quite contrary to his views on what should be done.

The secretary-general, with the help of the deputy-secretary-general, is dependent on this structure for the management of the United Nations Organization and for the implementation of the substantive policies for which he (or she) is held generally responsible by Member States. This includes the servicing of the many intergovernmental organs and bodies of the UN.

In summary, the main elements of the UN bureaucratic structure on which the secretary-general must depend are:

- A Secretariat staff of some 14,000 employees widely dispersed around the world.
- Eight departments in the Secretariat (at the latest count), headed by under-secretaries-general.
- A covey of senior advisors, special representatives, speech writers, and protocol functionaries in his immediate office, a growth area under recent secretaries-general.
- A sizeable number of separate functional and substantive support offices dealing with economic and social matters over some of which the secretary-general exercises only tenuous authority.[6]

THE SECRETARIAT STAFF

Each secretary-general has insisted on his right to control the formulation and implementation of personnel policy. This has been seen as essential for efficient administration and for the protection of the independence of the international civil service. As a result, personnel, or human resources management as it is now termed, is undoubtedly the administrative area in which the secretary-general has the greatest power. He has supreme authority to appoint, transfer, and dismiss staff members of the Secretariat. This is highly important for his ability to manage the organization, for respect of his authority within the Secretariat, and for his relations with Member States. Yet his control is far from complete.

The wage scales of Secretariat staff members are established by the General Assembly and are not subject to adjustment by the secretary-general. So, too, are important aspects of the retirement system. If employees demand higher wages or benefits, it is up to the assembly to grant or deny them. In 1978 the General Assembly resolved that by 1982 25 percent of all professional posts in the Secretariat subject to geographic distribution should be held by women. In 1980 the assembly went further, asking the secretary-general to examine additional measures to advance the attainment of policy directives in this area, including the possibility of designating a senior official to coordinate these functions. On another occasion the assembly resolved that a staff member should on transfer or retirement be replaced by a person of the same nationality if the representation in the Secretariat of his or her country was below the median of the desirable range for that country. In the face of an increasing tendency on the part of the assembly to legislate conditions of recruitment and service in the Secretariat, Secretary-General Kurt Waldheim and Secretary-General Javier Pérez de Cuéllar each warned against encroachment by the General Assembly on their authority in this area.

A secretary-general also faces continuing interference from Member States on personnel matters. Almost immediately after the first secretary-general assumed his post, the Soviet foreign minister informed him that the five Permanent Members of the Security Council had agreed that a Soviet national should be appointed as assistant-secretary-general for political and Security Council affairs. The U.S. secretary of state subsequently confirmed this, adding that the Big Five had decided to ask that a national of each be appointed as assistant-secretary-general. Lie comments in his memoirs that "by the terms of the Charter, the Secretary-General has full authority in the disposition of the assistant-secretary-generalships. . . . Strictly speaking, therefore, the Big Five had no right to arrive at any understanding regarding the distribution of offices. . . . This is not to say, however, that it would have been politic of me to resist the great-power accord."[7] So it has remained until the present time. The only difference is that the rank has advanced from assistant-secretary-general to under-secretary-general. The Permanent Members have frequently insisted not just that one of their nationals be appointed as under-secretary-general but that a particular person be given a specific post. When Boutros-Ghali became secretary-general he suggested in various statements that he would not be bound by consideration of nationality in the appointment of senior staff. He switched the posts occupied by representatives of the five Permanent Members—the United States, for example, was given the top administrative post rather than responsibility for the General Assembly. With the collapse of the Soviet Union, Moscow had to be content with an under-secretary-general position in Geneva. But all five retained posts at the under-secretary-general level. Moreover, Boutros-Ghali three times accepted the specific U.S. nominee for the crucial post of under-secretary-general for administration and management, two of whom proved unsatisfactory.

Pressure on personnel appointments is not limited to the five Permanent Members of the Security Council. Few countries refrain from it. The regional groups can be especially persistent on the ground of achieving equitable senior-level representation.

The secretary-general also faces a number of restrictions on the exercise of his authority in the form of the internal rules and regulations of the Secretariat. For example, all proposed recruitment below the senior director level (D-2) must be reviewed by one of the two appointment and promotion bodies. As part of the review process, the files of all staff members who might be qualified for the position are considered. In addition the status of the national quota of any proposed recruit is considered because, according to personnel guidelines, a person from a country that is overrepresented is not to be hired unless it can be demonstrably shown that no qualified candidate is available from a country that is not overrepresented. Because of these restrictions, a secretary-general may find it impossible to obtain the services of a person he considers best qualified to fill a particular post. The secretary-general legally can overrule the appointment and promotion bodies, but in doing so he would be going against a procedure introduced to ensure fairness in staff management and would be subject to criticism both within and outside the Secretariat for mismanagement. In his 1983 Annual Report to the General Assembly, Pérez de Cuéllar stated, "Very often I find myself caught between the directives of the General Assembly, the interests of the staff and the imperatives of good and efficient administration."[8] Such restrictive practices do not fit easily with an activist leadership of a United Nations facing the many challenges of the post–cold war world.

FURTHER LIMITATIONS ON THE SECRETARY-GENERAL'S FREEDOM OF ACTION

In his definitive lecture "The International Civil Servant in Law and in Fact," Dag Hammarskjöld noted that in Article 97 of the Charter the secretary-general is described as the "chief administrative officer of the organization," a phrase not found in the Covenant of the League of Nations. "Its explicit inclusion in the Charter," he stated, "made it a constitutional requirement—not simply a matter left to the discretion of the organs—that the administration of the Organization shall be left to the Secretary-General."[9] It is a constitutional provision that neither Member States individually nor the General Assembly has always honored. In a lecture in the same Oxford forum some twenty-five years later, Secretary-General Pérez de Cuéllar commented, "It would be a refreshing change if the General Assembly and individual Member States were to exercise more forbearance and give the Secretary-General the flexibility he needs to ensure the smooth and efficient functioning of the Secretariat."[10]

As noted earlier, the secretary-general was authorized by the first session of the General Assembly to make such changes in the original structure of the Secretariat as may be required to achieve the most effective distribution of responsibilities and functions. Thus the secretary-general *does* have the power to restructure the Secretariat. For example, Secretary-General Waldheim was responsible for establishing the Centre for Social Development in Vienna (mainly to provide occupants for the huge building that the Austrian government had built there for international agencies). Boutros-Ghali moved most of it back to New York. Pérez de Cuéllar established the Office for Research and the Collection of Information (ORCI) without reference to the General Assembly. Several Member States at first questioned this action because of perceived political implications, but none went so far as to challenge the right of the secretary-general to take it. However, he was only able to establish the office on the basis of existing resources. All posts and personnel had to be transferred from other offices; no outside recruitment was possible. Any additional expenditure for a new office would require the authorization of the General Assembly.

The secretary-general cannot on his authority establish new posts if there is no provision for them in the budget as approved by the General Assembly. Even to transfer posts from one section of the budget to another requires the approval of the Advisory Committee on Administrative and Budgetary Questions (ACABQ). The General Assembly declined to authorize additional posts for a policy advisory staff even though the staff was included in Secretary-General Annan's ambitious reform program, which the General Assembly had warmly endorsed. Before any request for additional resources is made to the assembly, it is reviewed by a Secretariat body responsible for program planning, where the request is assessed in terms of the program budget. When Secretary-General Pérez de Cuéllar wrote personally to the board recommending that provision be made in the next program budget for additional posts in ORCI to enhance his preventive diplomacy capabilities, the recommendation was rejected. The secretary-general can overrule such decisions, but this means disregarding the advice of an instrumentality established specifically to see to it that program priorities are respected in the allocation of budgetary resources. Many other examples could be cited that would illustrate the same realities: (1) a secretary-general can alter the structure of the Secretariat, and this has frequently been done; (2) if additional resources are involved, the authorization of the General Assembly is required and this is not always forthcoming; (3) likewise, any move to strengthen an existing program through additional resources requires the approval of the General Assembly; and (4) there are restrictions on the secretary-general's freedom to reallocate posts from one section of the budget without the concurrence of ACABQ.

The secretary-general, for better or worse, is not the only one who can alter the structure of the Secretariat. The General Assembly, as has been seen, approved the original structure of the Secretariat and it has, ever since, felt free to initiate organizational changes that have directly impacted the structure of the Secretariat and the management responsibility of the chief administrative officer. One example: In 1977 the assembly, acting on the basis of recommendations made by a committee of experts on the economic and social sectors, established the post of director-general for development and international economic co-operation as the second highest post in the Secretariat. The purpose was to give strong intellectual leadership to the economic programs of the entire UN system, in particular through effective interagency and interdisciplinary coordination. However, as Brian Urquhart and Erskine Childers have pointed out in a Ford Foundation study, the General Assembly left the new director-general and his office without the authority or the means to fulfill the mandate that the assembly had established.[11]

This is not to say that the secretary-general is without influence on such developments. His opinion is always sought. In this particular case Secretary-General Waldheim strongly opposed a proposal that the director-general be elected by the General Assembly for fear that the presence of a second elected official in the Secretariat would prejudice his own authority. Secretary-General Boutros-Ghali assumed the power to eliminate the position of director-general as part of his initial reform effort. His action was not challenged by the General Assembly even though it had created the position.

The group of high-level intergovernmental experts (Group of Eighteen) who in 1986 made extensive recommendations for reform of the administrative and financial functioning of the United Nations discreetly made their proposals available to the secretary-general for comment before they were finalized. Indeed, the group was unable to agree on perhaps the most sensitive question—namely, the size of the recommended cuts in the Secretariat staff—without an indication of what the secretary-general considered feasible. The chairman of the Group obtained the secretary-general's view in strict confidence, and the figure that the secretary-general named became the recommendation of the group.

So the secretary-general can exert very considerable influence on the decisions of the General Assembly affecting the structure of the Secretariat. The fact remains, however, that the secretary-general cannot control such decisions, which can have a very direct bearing on his management of the organization. This problem has assumed greater importance as priorities have shifted in recent years, demanding urgent shifts in personnel and resources to peacekeeping and peacemaking.

It is widely expected that the secretary-general should coordinate the administrative practices and the substantive programs of the entire UN system, including the specialized agencies. Yet nowhere in the Charter is this listed as one of his functions. As chief administrative officer he has authority over all elements of the United Nations Organization (the structure of which was described earlier) but not over the system as a whole. As has been indicated, his control over such semiautonomous functional offices as UNDP, UNICEF, and the United Nations Environment Program (UNEP) is nominal, deriving, to the extent it exists, from the fact that he designates or nominates the head of the office. The UN specialized agencies, of which there are sixteen, (for example, the World Health Organization, the World Bank, and the United Nations Educational, Scientific, and Cultural Organization), are completely independent and are not, even in theory, subject to the administrative supervision of the UN secretary-general. He has no influence on the selection of their executive heads.

Under Article 63 of the Charter, the Economic and Social Council (ECOSOC) is authorized to coordinate the activities of the specialized agencies through consultations and recommendations. The article makes no mention of the secretary-general. As noted earlier, Article 98 of the Charter provides that the secretary-general shall perform such functions as the principal organs entrust to him. It can be construed that the secretary-general, in efforts to coordinate the work of the system, is acting on behalf of ECOSOC. To accomplish this, as Secretary-General Boutros-Ghali vigorously set out to do, he must rely on his status as first among equals in relation to the executive heads of the specialized agencies, his chairmanship of the CEB, and his powers of persuasion. These are weak tools to achieve the kind of coordination that the system badly needs if their combined reserves are to contribute with maximum effectiveness to the tasks of conflict deterrence and peace-building that are increasingly viewed as essential UN goals.

To summarize, each secretary-general faces, to a greater or lesser extent, the following major administrative handicaps, which assume even greater importance as the responsibilities of the United Nations and the expectations placed in it have expanded.

1. Interference by Member States in personnel management, having as one result the placement of unqualified personnel in senior positions

2. A shortage of resources needed for the regular administrative costs of the organization and of humanitarian and security programs

3. A general lack of managerial ability and training among a culturally diverse Secretariat staff

4. Insufficient authority to achieve coordination among the functional offices and programs and the specialized agencies of the UN system

THE PROBLEM OF MONEY

The power to approve the budget of the United Nations rests entirely with the General Assembly. It also determines how the costs will be apportioned among Member States. The responsibility of the secretary-general is to propose and support, on a biannual basis, a budget that will provide the resources needed for the various programs of the organization. He operated for most of the 1990s and into the new millennium under the injunction of producing a no-growth budget. His proposal for the 2004–2006 biennium will show minor real growth. Once the biennium budget is approved by the General Assembly, the secretary-general must manage the United Nations within its financial and organizational limits. A relatively modest contingency fund is included to meet unexpected emergencies. Otherwise the secretary-general has little flexibility in increasing resources for programs he may wish to initiate or in transferring resources between programs. As the originator and lobbyist for the biennial budget the secretary-general can and does have major influence on the appropriation and allocation of resources. But the assembly frequently modifies his program proposals. The system thus imposes severe restraints on his freedom of action as senior manager.

The United Nations has a budget for the regular expenditures of the organization and separate budgets for each peacekeeping operation. Each Member State is assessed on the basic principle of ability to pay, with some allowance given to population and extreme poverty. The five Permanent Members of the Security Council are assessed a slightly higher percentage for peacekeeping budgets than for the regular budget. The United States has always been the highest contributor.

Beginning as early as the peacekeeping operation in the Sinai in 1956 (UNEF I), a number of countries began to withhold a small portion of their assessed contributions for political reasons. This first reached crisis proportions at the time of the Congo operation in the 1960s, when both the Soviet Union and France withheld their assessed payments on questions of principle. The Soviet arrears eventually exceeded two years of its assessed contributions, thus making it liable to the loss of its vote in the General Assembly under Article 19 of the Charter. Through a compromise worked out between the United States and the Soviet Union, the Soviets retained their vote (without paying the arrears), but the UN faced the prospect of bankruptcy. Secretary-General Hammarskjöld sought the advice of U.S. bankers, who advised that the UN sell bonds. The immediate crisis was thus solved, but the ability of the secretary-general to maintain the Congo peace operation had been seriously threatened.

A new crisis began in the 1980s when the U.S. Congress passed legislation requiring that the United States withhold 20 percent of its regular assessed contribution until the General Assembly agreed that all resolutions dealing with UN financing be subject to weighted voting. While this requirement was eventually repealed, other restrictions were added, and to show dissatisfaction with UN peacekeeping operations and the UN in general, the U.S. Congress failed to appropriate funds to cover a substantial part of the U.S. assessments. Beginning with Secretary-General Pérez de Cuéllar, each secretary-general was required to spend enormous time and energy in trying to persuade Washington to pay its bill, which by 2000 was well over one billion dollars according to UN calculations. As a result of the shortage of funds, peacekeeping operations for which the secretary-general was responsible were delayed; others that the secretary-general recommended were either not implemented or not given sufficient resources to be effective. UN property, including the headquarters building in New York, fell into disrepair, and it appeared at times that the secretary-general would not be able to meet the payroll of his staff. In response to the extensive reforms introduced by Secretary-General Annan—partly to meet U.S. demands—the United States agreed to pay a major portion of its arrears if its assessment for the regular budget were reduced from 25 percent to 22 percent and its peacekeeping assessment from just over 30 percent to 25 percent. After the General Assembly agreed to the 22 percent regular budget assessment and to a reduction to 26.5 percent for peacekeeping budgets, the United States paid a substantial portion of its arrears and most of its current assessments.[12] The secretary-general is constricted both in substantive policies and administrative management by such severe, externally imposed limitations on the availability and utilization of resources.

UNITED NATIONS REFORM

Criticism of the administration of the United Nations has been over the years a continuing phenomenon. As set forth in innumerable internal and external reports, it has been sustained and unvarnished relating to such purely administrative matters as financial management and personnel policies as well as to the conduct of substantive programs such as peacekeeping and economic development. The Group of Eighteen in 1986 concluded that "management capacity, especially with regard to the need to maintain overall administrative efficiency, productivity and cost effectiveness, has lagged behind [the] pace of growth. The quality of work needs to be improved upon. The qualifications of staff, in particular in the higher categories, are inadequate and the working methods are not efficient. Today's structure is too complex, fragmented and top-heavy."[13] As a result of various reform initiatives over the years both the Security Council and ECOSOC have been enlarged and the latter subjected to altered schedules and agendas. Budget and staff growth since the late 1980s has been held in check; administrative economies have been introduced; and controversies over the budget have been reduced with the introduction in 1987 of decision on the regular UN budget by consensus. Limited rationalization of procedures in the General Assembly and the Security Council has been effected. But whatever the benefit of these changes, they were not sufficient to quell a chorus of demands for further reform as necessary to enhance the effectiveness of the United Nations in the post–cold war era and to equip it to deal with the challenges of the twenty-first century. When the General Assembly met at the summit level in 1995 to commemorate the fiftieth anniversary of the founding of the United Nations, practically every government leader insisted first that the United Nations was indispensable, and second that it was badly in need of reform.

When Annan became secretary-general at the beginning of 1997 he responded to these presentations and the many recommendations for reform that had been put forward by private groups by making reform an immediate and central objective. In his 1997 report to the General Assembly entitled "Renewing the United Nations: A Programme for Reform," he stated that "reform is not an event; it is a process."[14] The following are the more important recommendations included in the reform program that have been implemented:

- Establishment of the post of Deputy-Secretary-General.

- Establishment of four Executive Committees to bring together all Secretariat departments, programs, and funds in dealing with the core missions of the UN: peace and security, economic and social affairs, development operations, and humanitarian affairs, with human rights as a cross-cutting issue.

- Establishment of a Senior Management Group to assist the secretary-general in achieving unity of purpose and direction in the work of the UN.

- Consolidation of the three departments dealing with economic and social matters into a single Department of Economic and Social Affairs.

- Establishment of a Strategic Planning Unit to provide the secretary-general with policy-relevant information and research.

- Consolidation of the Office of the High Commissioner for Human Rights and the Center for Human Rights.

- Consolidation in a single office in Vienna of UN programs for combating crime, drugs, and terrorism.

- Enhancement of the UN's capacity to respond faster to sudden emergencies including, inter alia, the training of military and civilian participants in peacekeeping exercises.

- Establishment in each field post of common premises—a "UN House"—for all UN programs.

- Designation of a United Nations Humanitarian Assistance Coordinator and the establishment of a humanitarian affairs segment of ECOSOC.

- Adoption of a "budgeting for results" system characterized by accountability for results rather than inputs.

- Adoption of a code of conduct for UN staff members. A code of conduct was not adopted under that name but various principles included in a draft developed by the secretary-general have been incorporated in the official staff rules and regulations. In addition, the secretary-general called for a rejuvenation of the Secretariat (without specifying how) and the examination by a task force of experts of the entire approach to human resources, which he considered both "ineffective and inefficient."

The secretary-general made a number of other recommendations, the more interesting of which are listed below, that were either not approved by the General Assembly or could not be implemented for other reasons.

- Reconstitution of the Trusteeship Council as the forum through which Member States could exercise their collective trusteeship for the global environment and the global commons. Because General Assembly agreement could not be reached on this recommendation, the Trusteeship Council remains unchanged and essentially unemployed.

- Consolidation and reconfiguration of ECOSOC's subsidiary bodies. No specific organizational changes resulted from this recommendation but, in the spirit of the reform movement, working practices in many of these bodies have become more open, informal, and generally productive.

- Development of a rapidly deployable military-civilian mission headquarters for peacekeeping operations; the establishment of a time frame for the conclusion of status-of-forces agreements for peacekeeping operations, and, pending such agreements, the provisional application of a model status-of-forces agreement. While the assembly endorsed these recommendations, financial and political difficulties have prevented agreement on a rapidly deployable mission headquarters. A model status-of-forces agreement remains under study.

- The establishment of a development account to be funded from possible savings in the program budget for 1998–99. The assembly accepted this recommendation but not the elimination of programs on which the savings depended. The development account has therefore remained inactive.

Almost all of these recommendations were intended to give the secretary-general new means of obtaining better coordination and avoiding duplication among the various UN agencies and programs and of improving the efficiency of the UN staff. Rather than visionary, the recommendations were pragmatic, intended to meet urgent and practical problems. Those that have been implemented have had good results. They have produced a more flexible and open organization, better able to undertake complex humanitarian, development, and peace-building operations because of greater internal cooperation and systemwide unity of purpose. The U.S. Congress found them sufficient to warrant release of a substantial portion of the unpaid U.S. dues.

WHAT A SECRETARY-GENERAL NEEDS

Repeated secretaries-general have said that the only power they possess is the moral power that derives from the UN Charter, which they represent. This is not quite true. A secretary-general is expected to play many roles: manager, commander of peacekeeping operations, mediator, communicator, statesman, and spokesperson for the United Nations. In each of these capacities, the secretary-general can have an impact on world affairs. The impact depends not just on the moral principles that he or she represents but also on his or her personal qualities and on the effective operation of the organization that he or she leads. The qualities that are most important for a secretary-general are high intelligence; managerial ability; good judgment; trustworthiness; the absence of personal prejudices; expertise in international political, social, and economic affairs; and outstanding communication skills. No secretary-general is likely to be endowed with all these qualities in equal measure. He or she is certain to need the assistance of a competent and loyal staff. Management skill is needed at every level. Management capacity has two dimensions. One is the skill to run an office, to give effective supervision to subordinate staff, to keep a tight budget, and so on—in other words, administration in a strict sense. The other dimension is that of *executive leadership,* or macromanagement. In considering the role of the secretary-general this distinction is important. The secretary-general can now rely on the deputy-secretary-general for strong support in the exercise of executive leadership, which represents a major step forward in achieving a well-coordinated UN organization. Below this level, however, management skills are uneven and have lagged behind the enlarged operational requirements of the United Nations. More extensive training programs can alleviate this problem. Such programs have been undertaken, largely financed on a voluntary basis by Japan. This has helped. However, many of the higher-level posts are filled by persons recruited at a senior rank from varied managerial cultures who assume managerial responsibility without the possibility of midcareer training. The only solution for this, and it is not likely to be entirely satisfactory, is for the secretary-general to insist on demonstrated managerial capacity in the selection of occupants for these posts.

To lead the United Nations effectively, the secretary-general needs good relations with the Permanent Members, one concomitant of which is the presence of their nationals in senior Secretariat positions. Persons appointed with the strong backing of a government can on occasion serve as a useful channel for the secretary-general to that government in connection with both administrative and substantive responsibilities. However, the secretary-general must be prepared to resist strong pressure from a Permanent Member in behalf of a favored candidate if he or she finds the candidate unsuitable. In addition to insisting on the submission of more than one candidate, the secretary-general can also insist on freedom to decide which post is to be filled by each country.

Wide geographic representation at the most senior levels is obviously desirable. It is not something that a secretary-general would wish to resist. It is not easy, however, to identify the right person from a large geographic region to fill a particular post. The secretary-general, to meet successfully the demands of this aspect of the managerial responsibility, needs the assistance of a kind of international headhunters group. It would be advisable for the secretary-general, or the under-secretary-general for administration and management on his behalf, to establish an informal advisory group on whose members he or she could call in confidence to help find the best-qualified person in a particular region who might be available for a senior UN post.

Closely related to the managerial task of obtaining a thoroughly competent senior staff is the responsibility to create a structure that will encourage the staff to make their full contribution to the attainment of the goals of the organization. This means opening as many doors as possible to a sense of participation by a broad range of Secretariat personnel in the substantive work in which the secretary-general is engaged directly. As chief administrative officer, the secretary-general needs to instill a sense of participation and purpose throughout the staff of the organization. A compartmentalization that has grown increasingly rigid over the years has worked against this in the United Nations. It was not alleviated by the seemingly arbitrary changes that Secretary-General Boutros-Ghali made in the Secretariat. But Annan, coming into the post of secretary-general from the Secretariat staff, has taken steps to alleviate the problem through greater interchange among the departments. Still, the problem remains. The opportunity for field service in operations such as Namibia, Central America, Cambodia, Bosnia, and East Timor has served to reinvigorate staff members by taking them out of the strict confines of departments or offices and allowing them to work on an important undertaking as part of an interdisciplinary UN team. With the many cross-disciplinary threats to global security, a comparable team approach should be encouraged at the major UN centers.

In an era when communication is of paramount importance, the United Nations long remained notably lacking in communication skills. With the advent of Annan, the UN for the first time gained a leader of extraordinary public relations ability. He has personally taken the lead in explaining to governments and the world public the validity and the necessity of new as well as traditional UN approaches in meeting the challenges of the present era. The secretary-general must more than ever articulate the substantive objectives in which the whole UN system should be joined and bring leadership and coordination to their pursuit. The power of persuasion can and should be an important power in the hands of a secretary-general. Even a person as gifted as Annan cannot do this work alone. Well aware of this, Annan (and the General Assembly as well) has insisted on a major restructuring of the Department of Public Information (DPI), which is responsible for bringing news of UN programs and activities to world attention. In addition, he has placed a close and highly articulate associate in charge of the department who, against considerable odds, has brought greater cohesion and transparency to the department's multiple mandated programs.

The process of peace-building and the transitional administration of territories or countries in which the United Nations is engaged requires the combined support of various UN programs such as UNHCR and UNDP and also of UN specialized agencies such as the World Food Program, the World Bank, and the World Health Organization over which the secretary-general has no control. Annan has brought about a closer coordination and planning relationship among the semi-independent programs that fall within his jurisdiction and his office. The deputy-secretary-general has been given oversight responsibility in this area. The secretary-general has also reached out to the heads of the specialized agencies and has developed a closer working relationship with them on specific problems and projects. The relationship remains less than satisfactory, however. The leadership role of the secretary-general in systemwide planning and policy development needs greater recognition and respect. This will have to be on a voluntary basis, as none of the specialized agencies is inclined to relinquish its independent status.

THE SAFETY OF UN PERSONNEL

Given the prevalence of volatile political situations in countries where United Nations humanitarian or assistance programs are under way, UN personnel and affiliated NGO staff members often find themselves in grave and sudden danger. In the absence of protection, the only conscionable action for the secretary-general to take, given his responsibility for the safety of UN staff members, is to withdraw the UN personnel and thereby interrupt what may be gravely needed help for a civilian population under threat. In such cases, it would be of both humanitarian and morale value if the secretary-general had the authority and the contingency budget quickly to send a UN guard contingent adequately trained and armed to afford protection to the UN and, to the extent possible, other international humanitarian personnel present in the area.

There are precedents for such action. Trygve Lie, the first secretary-general, after his proposal to form a UN constabulary force had been turned down, sent UN guards to provide protection for UN personnel in Palestine at the time of the first Arab-Israeli war. More recently (and more relevantly) Secretary-General Pérez de Cuéllar sent UN guards to Northern Iraq, where the United Nations was seeking to bring humanitarian relief to the Kurdish population, which was under attack from the Iraqi government. Some members of the Security Council had urged that a UN peacekeeping force be sent to the area. The Iraqi authorities refused to give their consent. The secretary-general therefore proposed, instead, to send UN guards to the area. The guards were ostensibly to provide protection for UN relief centers and UN personnel, but it was also intended that their presence give a sense of security to the Kurdish population. The Iraqis agreed that the guards could be deployed, carrying only side arms. Some 600 were eventually deployed (some were stationed at other points in Iraq) to very good effect both in terms of the safety of UN personnel and of the sense of greater security enjoyed by the Kurds.

Secretary-General Pérez de Cuéllar sent the guards on his own authority. The Security Council had passed a resolution demanding that Iraq allow access to all residents in need of humanitarian assistance. This was seen as a legal justification for the secretary-general's action, although the legal staff of the Secretariat has never given an opinion on whether such justification was necessary. UN guards have the status of regular Secretariat staff members. As such they are subject to assignment by the secretary-general to any UN post. They would be recruited by the United Nations and not provided by contributing countries. Training would be done by the UN. When not needed in emergencies, they could supplement the guard contingents at regular posts or be integrated for special police duties in peacekeeping operations. As was the case in Iraq, local authorities are likely to be more amenable to the dispatch of UN guards than to military peacekeeping personnel.

THE POWER OF THE GENERAL ASSEMBLY

Greater authorization to move positions within the Secretariat and the establishment of a standing UN guard contingent available for use in emergencies by the secretary-general are two relatively modest ways in which the authority of the secretary-general could be enlarged to give him or her a greater capability to deal with the increasingly demanding problems faced by the UN. Neither would involve any Charter modification.

Having said this, it must be added that members have traditionally been reluctant to see the power of the secretary-general increased. The one suggestion that Secretary-General Boutros-Ghali made in *An Agenda for Peace* that would have slightly enhanced his authority by empowering him to refer a matter to the International Court of Justice was simply ignored by Member States. It is by no means certain that there would be approval in the General Assembly even for the steps proposed here.

For the most part, the present secretary-general, Annan, and most likely his successors, will have to fulfill the complex responsibilities of the post–cold war era through skillful utilization of existing authority and through the strength of their resolve, the force of their personality, and their communication skills. With these qualities a secretary-general can counter, or overcome, many of the obstacles that are an inherent part of the job. There is one, in particular, however, that no secretary-general will be able to resolve on his own—the obstacle that inadequate resources constitutes for the successful management of the organization and its programs. A substantial number of additional posts were authorized for the Department of Peacekeeping Affairs in the 2000–2001 budget. Major additions in permanent staff may not be necessary to cover regular programs. However, additional funding will be needed to allow the secretary-general flexibility in the prudent maintenance of UN property and in the deployment and maintenance of peace operations. The funds available for peacekeeping have been dangerously insufficient, to the point that when deployment of a peacekeeping force to Bosnia was agreed upon in 1992, the secretary-general was forced to say that there were no funds available for the action and therefore those countries participating would have to cover their own expenses. If funds are inadequate, the secretary-general cannot manage the deployment of a peacekeeping operation in such a way as to ensure its timely effectiveness. The resource problem extends to the whole area of peace-building, where the secretary-general is unable to implement the programs needed for building democratic institutions if sufficient funding is not available. In the end, the successful fulfillment of the secretary-general's responsibilities as chief administrative officer under the Charter depends heavily on the willingness of Member States to provide adequate resources in a timely manner.

NOTES

1. Dick Thornburgh, "Report to the Secretary-General of the United Nations" dated 1 March 1993 (unpublished); made available by Mr. Thornburgh.

2. Ruth B. Russell, *A History of the United Nations Charter* (Washington, D.C.: Brookings Institution, 1958), p. 371.

3. General Assembly Official Records: forty-first session, Supplement No. 49 (a/41/49).

4. As of 2001, the UN Secretariat included 7,485 personnel paid from the regular assessed budget and 7,389 paid from extrabudgetary resources, making a total of 14,874.

5. The Economic and Social Commission for West Asia now located in Amman earlier had its headquarters in Baghdad and may return there when conditions are appropriate.

6. In their study "The Reorganization of the United Nations Secretariat," written in February 1991, Brian Urquhart and Erskine Childers state that more than thirty units in the Secretariat are supposed to report directly to the secretary-general.

7. Trygve Lie, *In the Cause of Peace* (New York: Macmillan, 1954), p. 45.

8. Report of the Secretary-General on the Work of the Organization, in Javier Pérez de Cuéllar, *Anarchy or Order* (New York: United Nations, 1983), p. 21.

9. Dag Hammarskjöld, *The International Civil Servant in Law and in Fact* (Oxford: Clarendon Press, 1961).

10. Lecture delivered by Secretary-General Pérez de Cuéllar at Oxford University, 13 April 1986.

11. See Urquhart and Childers, *A World in Need of Leadership* (Uppsala, Sweden: Dag Hammarskjöld Foundation, 1996), p. 83.

12. For a comprehensive discussion of present UN assessment scales, see Jeffrey Laurenti, *The New UN Assessment Scale* (New York: UNA/USA, 1998).

13. General Assembly Official Records: forty-first session, Supplement No. 49 (a/41/49).

14. UN document A/51/950 (1997), paragraph 25.

Chapter 9

THE CHALLENGE FOR GOVERNMENTS AND PEOPLES

In discussions and studies of the ability of the United Nations to meet the challenge of maintaining international security in the circumstances of an essentially new era, there is a frequent tendency to look at the organization as a self-contained entity, to be praised or condemned as if it could correct inadequacies and acquire new capabilities through its own means. The undertaking or nonundertaking of humanitarian intervention operations, the application of sanctions to induce compliance with Security Council resolutions, the restructuring of the UN system—such actions are usually portrayed as dependent on the UN secretary-general, the Security Council, or one of the other UN organs. Such an impression might well be gained from what is recorded in some of the preceding chapters, which have focused on the UN's organization and on the secretary-general. But this is not so. The ability of the United Nations to meet adequately the demands placed on it by present world conditions depends heavily on decisions of governments and on the attitudes and orientation of populations on which governmental policies are ultimately dependent. In searching for answers on how the capacity of the United Nations to contribute to the maintenance of international security can be enhanced, it is necessary to look beyond the UN headquarters building in New York to national capitals and to world public opinion.

A critical issue, alluded to earlier, that will affect the capacity of the

United Nations to provide security for populations under threat is that of national sovereignty. This issue has been clearly posed by the humanitarian and political crises that have occurred and continue to occur within countries in various regions of the world. All recent secretaries-general have tried to define a policy on this issue. All have said in differing words that to stand back and do nothing in the face of genocide or crimes against humanity would be obscene but to disregard the sovereign rights of states would spell chaos. Secretary-General Kofi Annan has gone further than his predecessors in holding that concern for the well-being of threatened people or individuals should take precedence over the restrictions on action inherent in total respect for sovereignty. But a secretary-general can only recommend. As influential as that may be, governments must still decide if, and under what circumstances, the UN can intervene in the internal affairs of states. Action has been taken by the Security Council in Somalia, Central America, the former Yugoslavia, East Timor, and elsewhere that suggests the international community is moving toward a flexible interpretation of the limitations that sovereignty imposes on intervention in the domestic affairs of a country. However, widespread resistance among Member States is also evident.

The action taken by the United Nations has therefore been halting, inconsistent, and at times shamefully inadequate. This is mainly because there is no clarity among states as to what is possible or desirable in terms of UN intervention or how many resources they are prepared to provide if action is taken. After the fighting in the Gulf War was over, the Iraqi government took oppressive measures against the Kurdish minority in the north and the Shiite minority in the south that threatened, especially in the case of the Kurds, to amount to genocide. In the face of this massive violation of human rights the Security Council demanded that Iraq immediately end the repression of the civilian population "as a contribution to removing the threat to international peace and security." In the same resolution, however, the council reaffirmed the commitment of all Member States "to the sovereignty, territorial integrity and political independence of Iraq."[1] When Secretary-General Javier Pérez de Cuéllar was urged to arrange for the dispatch of a peacekeeping force to afford protection to the Kurds, he concluded that under the terms of the resolution it could only be done with the consent of the Iraqi government, which the Iraqi regime refused to give. The U.S., British, and French governments then intervened militarily to establish a protected zone in the north and, subsequently, in the south in evident contravention of Iraq's sovereignty. Acting on the premise that respect for sovereignty required the consent of the government, the UN sent guards to Iraq only after the concurrence of Iraqi authorities had been obtained to afford protection, theoretically, only to UN personnel and installations but, in practice, also to the local population. The wording of the resolution and the differing approaches of the three powers and of the UN to intervention are indicative of the ambivalent attitudes of governments on the relative priority to be given the protection of human rights and the protection of sovereignty. In an age of transparency this is an issue on which decisions of governments (and UN action) will be heavily influenced by popular attitudes—by revulsion over the suffering of fellow human beings revealed daily and graphically on television and also by reluctance to see sons and daughters placed in harm's way to protect the human rights of people far from their native shores.

It is governments, too, that will need to make the decisions on the extent to which the United Nations, acting in their behalf, should be involved in nation building where, through civil war or criminal leadership, governance has collapsed. Governments are inclined to insist on exit strategies if peace-building operations are proposed. More apposite would be the development of a strategy before such an operation begins for staying as long as necessary to see the instrumentalities of democratic governance and economic development firmly in place. This will provide the best assurance that internal peace will be sustained and that the country will assume a constructive role in world society.

Also in the case of basic organizational changes in the UN system, only governments can make the necessary decisions. Secretaries-general have altered the structure of the Secretariat by creating or eliminating offices, reapportioning functions, and generally "moving boxes" on an organizational chart. However, no secretary-general or Secretariat task force can alter the composition of the Security Council to make it more representative or revise the decentralized structure of the UN system to permit greater policy direction for the central UN organs. Basic decisions remain to be made in these areas to equip the United Nations to meet adequately the clash between globalization and nationalism and the ever-greater disparity between rich and poor countries. In the case of the Security Council, decisions will lie primarily with the five Permanent Members without whose concurrence no change is possible. As a decision-making body with responsibility for the maintenance of peace and international security, the Security Council is unquestionably functioning more effectively now than ever before in its existence. It is difficult, and probably dangerous, to believe, however, that the authority of the council can be sustained indefinitely if the unrepresentative allocation of power to the present Permanent Members remains unchanged.

More immediately, the authority of the Security Council has been challenged by the decision of NATO powers, including three Permanent Members of the Security Council, to use military force against Serbia in Kosovo without authorization of the council. This action was taken in the face of the likelihood that Russia would veto any resolution endorsing a resort to military force under Chapter VII of the Charter. The NATO action was widely seen among Member States as justified in order to prevent a massive slaughter of Albanian residents of Kosovo. It received a form of post-facto endorsement since the council decided that the United Nations, working in tandem with NATO, would undertake responsibility for the peacebuilding process in Kosovo, including the transitional civil administration of the territory. Therefore, the Kosovo action was not interpreted as a serious blow to the competence of the United Nations.

A far more serious challenge was posed by the decision of the United States and the United Kingdom to wage war against Iraq in seeming defiance of the Security Council, in which three Permanent Members and a majority of nonpermanent members strongly opposed the action. The United States and the United Kingdom asserted that the action was taken in accordance with existing council resolutions adopted after Iraq's defeat in the Gulf War. This assertion was placed in question, however, by their intense efforts to obtain a further resolution specifically authorizing the military action. President George W. Bush on several occasions warned that the Security Council would become irrelevant if it did not authorize the use of all necessary means to force Saddam Hussein to relinquish once and for all Iraq's weapons of mass destruction capability. In fact the United Sates and the United Kingdom found it prudent to return to the council to seek legitimization of the provisional authority they had established as occupying powers to govern Iraq pending the establishment of an elected Iraqi government. The council complied and called on the secretary-general to resume the oil for food program (for six months) and send a personal envoy to Iraq to work with the authority in furthering the reconstruction of Iraq and the establishment of a democratic government. In this same time frame, the Security Council was called on to undertake peace enforcement action in the Democratic Republic of the Congo and only shortly thereafter in Liberia. These developments were proof enough that the Security Council had not been rendered irrelevant by the U.S.-led military action against Iraq. What was shown with brutal clarity was that the Security Council derives such power as it has from the unity of its Permanent Members. If this is absent, the Security Council becomes a weak instrument for the maintenance of international security.

Government decisions pertaining to the allocation of resources, both human and material, will have a fundamental effect on the success of the United Nations in maintaining international security in the future. The challenge facing the world community in this respect is most graphically evident in regard to peacekeeping and peace enforcement. The terms *peacekeeping* and *peace enforcement* are no longer adequate to describe the responsibilities undertaken by the United Nations in internal conflicts. *Peace operations* is a more accurate term because it can encompass activities ranging from traditional peacekeeping and peace enforcement to peacemaking and nation building. Such operations have become so demanding and complex as to outstrip the willingness and/or the capability of traditional sources to provide the needed personnel. The costs are so high as to meet increasing resistance of governments in making payments that they do not see as directly related to their national security, as traditionally understood. Moreover, the increased sensitivity and danger inherent in enforcement actions are causing reluctance on the part of governments to see their troops involved under UN command. This reluctance reflects public attitudes that, while generally in favor of peacekeeping, can quickly become negative in the face of media coverage of their soldiers being killed—or killing local nationals—on behalf of the vaguely understood concept of international security. When the Security Council resolved that an additional 7,500 troops should be sent to Bosnia to protect the safe areas designated by the council, the secretary-general found Member States reluctant to volunteer forces, and a considerable delay in their deployment resulted, notwithstanding the urgency of the need. This problem is sufficiently serious as to jeopardize the ability of the United Nations to take the forceful interventionist measures for peace that have become politically acceptable in the face of massive human rights abuse, genocide, and terrorism. A pattern has emerged, foreshadowed in the *Supplement* to Boutros Boutros-Ghali's *Agenda for Peace:* military enforcement action to end conflict is undertaken by NATO or coalitions of national armies, while the peace-building function, including civilian administration, is entrusted to the UN.[2] This only works in conflicts where the interests of militarily capable powers or regional organizations are engaged. Even then, the resources provided for the lengthy and complex peace-building process are often inadequate. If resources are to be provided in sufficient measure for purposes of human security, there will have to be a fundamental change in public and governmental perceptions in countries that are no longer directly or indirectly threatened by cold war rivalries. It must be accepted that while national defense establishments cannot be abandoned, the purposes they serve—and must be structured and trained to serve—include international *human* security. This means that major resource outlays and the acceptance of serious risks, until now justifiable only for national defense or directly related alliance defense, must become justifiable to afford safety to threatened peoples as a common human responsibility and a common human interest. Such a development can only come from a basic change in popular attitudes that will have its effect on parliamentary positions and government policies. What is in question is nothing less than a modification of the traditional understanding of the mission of national defense.

Some change is already apparent. As has been recorded earlier, the Security Council adopted, with the affirmative vote of France, Russia, the United Kingdom, and the United States, a resolution declaring that the humanitarian crisis in Somalia amounted to a threat to international security, warranting enforcement action to relieve it. The military enforcement action led by the United States, at considerable cost in defense resources, to provide security for humanitarian assistance in Somalia did not serve U.S. national defense, or the national defense of the twenty other countries that participated. Australia led a military action to restore peace in East Timor, where a massive abuse of human rights was taking place. The world community was generous in providing resources needed for nation building. More than any other development, global terrorism has brought many countries to realize that the traditional perception of the mission of national defense forces is no longer adequate. Canadians, for example, in and outside of government, have been seeking to redefine the function of the Canadian defense forces, and many, in so doing, have seen peacekeeping (including peace-building) as a major rationale for their retention.

The adequate allocation of resources for the purpose of building peace is, of course, a problem extending far beyond the defense field. The provision by developed countries of assistance for economic and social development, whether bilaterally or through multilateral organizations, has always been motivated and justified by the needs of the recipient as well as the interests of the donor. Still, the provision of foreign assistance even in limited amounts has never been popular with electorates outside the Nordic countries. The resources needed for humanitarian assistance and for economic and social development to build a sound basis for peace and human security are far in excess of what most governments in the developed world are likely to make available as matters now stand. With the greatly increased threat of terrorism in the world that was brought brutally to public consciousness by the terrorist attacks on the United States on September 11, 2001, a new factor has been introduced into the picture. It has been widely recognized that the fight against terrorism entails the allocation of far greater resources to the alleviation of poverty, to education, and improved health standards. The United States, long a laggard in the provision of international assistance, made an additional 5 billion dollars available for anti-AIDS programs as a means of attacking the causes of terrorism. But this is only one step toward a reordering of the global economy so that adequate resources are made available where they are most needed to strengthen the security and well-being of nations and individuals.

In 1983 the UN General Assembly created the World Commission on Environment and Development under the chairmanship of Norwegian prime minister Gro Harlem Brundtland and asked it to formulate a "global agenda for change."[3] This was the origin of the concept of sustainable development,[4] which has led to far-reaching changes in public attitudes and in governmental policies. The World Conference on the Environment that was held in Rio de Janeiro in 1992 did a great deal to encourage a new philosophy on the preservation of the environment as an integral element in development. It greatly influenced the development of the Kyoto Protocol setting limits on environmentally harmful emissions.

The goal of bringing about fundamental changes in public thinking and government policies on the mission of national defense establishments and on the allocation of resources in the interest of human security is breathtaking, and to many, no doubt, confounding. But the international constellation at present is unique in history both in the opportunities it offers to enhance international security and in the terrible evidence it displays, in the form of terrorism, civil wars, and genocide, of the dangers of not exploiting them. It was no doubt presumptuous of Presidents George Herbert Walker Bush and Mikhail Gorbachev to speak glowingly of a new world order without defining very clearly what it would be or providing useful guidance on how to get there. They were right, though, in sensing that great changes were in the making. The world has entered a new era. It would be an enduring tragedy if this new era were characterized by retrogression into chaos because national commitment and resources were not available in sufficient measure to enhance significantly human security or to afford the United Nations the credibility it must have if it is to be a major and effective force for democracy, development, and peace.

NOTES

1. S/RES/688 (1991).

2. The *Supplement* to *An Agenda for Peace* is included in the 1995 edition of *An Agenda for Peace* published by the United Nations.

3. A/RES/38/161 (1985).

4. See World Commission on Environment and Development, *Our Common Future: Report of the World Commission on Environment and Development* (New York: Oxford University Press, 1987).

SELECTED BIBLIOGRAPHY

Annan, Kofi A. *Prevention of Armed Conflict.* New York: United Nations, 2002.
———. *We the Peoples: The Role of the United Nations in the 21st Century.* New York: United Nations, 2000.

Baehr, Peter R., and Leon Gordenker. *The United Nations in the 1990s.* New York: St. Martin's Press, 1992.

Blechman, Barry M., and J. Matthew Vaccoro. *Training for Peacekeeping: The United Nations' Role.* Washington, D.C.: Henry L. Stimson Center, 1994.

Boulden, Jane. *Prometheus Unborn: The History of the Military Staff Committee.* Ottawa: Canadian Centre for Global Security, 1993.

Boutros-Ghali, Boutros. *An Agenda for Peace.* New York: United Nations, 1995.
———. *Report of the Secretary-General on the Work of the Organization to the Forty-seventh Session of the General Assembly.* New York: United Nations, 1992.

Claude, Inis L., Jr. *Swords into Plowshares.* New York: Random House, 1984.

Cox, David. *Exploring an Agenda for Peace.* Ottawa: Canadian Centre for Global Security, 1993.

Diehl, Paul F. *International Peacekeeping.* Baltimore, Md.: Johns Hopkins University Press, 1993.

Durch, William J. *The Evolution of UN Peacekeeping.* New York: St. Martin's Press, 1993.

Goodrich, Leland. *The Charter of the United Nations.* Boston: World Peace Foundation, 1949.

Gordenker, Leon, and Benjamin Rivlin, eds. *The Challenging Role of the UN Secretary-General.* Westport, Conn.: Praeger, 1993.

Kennedy, Paul. *Preparing for the Twenty-first Century.* New York: Random House, 1993.

Krasno, Jean E., and James S. Sutterlin. *The United Nations and Iraq: Defanging the Viper.* Westport, Conn.: Praeger, 2003.

Lie, Trygve. *In the Cause of Peace.* New York: Macmillan, 1954.

Pérez de Cuéllar, Javier. *Anarchy or Order.* New York: United Nations, 1991.

Report of the Panel on United Nations Peace Operations. UN Document A/55/305 (2000).

Russell, Ruth B. *A History of the United Nations Charter.* Washington, D.C.: Brookings Institution, 1958.

Russett, Bruce. *Grasping the Democratic Peace.* Princeton, N.J.: Princeton University Press, 1993.

Stettinius, Edward T., Jr. *Report to the President on the San Francisco Conference.* Washington, D.C.: U.S. Department of State, 26 June 1945.

United Nations. *The Blue Helmets.* New York: United Nations, 1996.

Urquhart, Brian. *Dag Hammarskjold.* New York: Harper and Row, 1984.

Wiess, Thomas G., ed. *Collective Security in a Changing World.* Boulder, Colo.: Lynne Rienner, 1993.

Williams, Douglas. *The Specialized Agencies and the United Nations.* London: Hurst, 1987.

World Commission on Environment and Development. *Our Common Future: Report of the World Commission on Environment and Development.* New York: Oxford University Press, 1987.

Index

About the Author

JAMES S. SUTTERLIN is Lecturer and Fellow in United Nations Studies at Yale University and Adjunct Professor at Long Island University. Following service in the U.S. Army during World War II, Sutterlin entered the Foreign Service with posts in Germany, Israel, Japan, and Washington. In 1974, Sutterlin joined the United Nations Secretariat, serving as a senior aide to the Secretary-General.